Citizens and Service Delivery

Citizens and Service Delivery

Assessing the Use of Social Accountability
Approaches in the Human Development Sectors

Dena Ringold
Alaka Holla
Margaret Koziol
Santhosh Srinivasan

THE WORLD BANK
Washington, D.C.

ISBN: 978-0-8213-8980-5
eISBN: 978-0-8213-8930-0
DOI: 10.1596/978-0-8213-8930-0

Library of Congress Cataloging-in-Publication Data has been applied for.

Cover design: Naylor Design, Washington, D.C.

Contents

Foreword

Efforts by governments, donors, and civil society alike to improve governance, accountability, and development results on the ground have heightened attention to the idea that citizens can contribute to better public services by holding their policy makers, providers, and program managers accountable. While the use of social accountability to improve services in low- and middle-income countries is not new, the topic has gained currency in recent years.

In particular, the *World Development Report 2004: Making Services Work for Poor People* provided a conceptual framework that has been influential through its emphasis on the capacity of individuals and communities, as users of services and as citizens, as a key force for change. The report catalyzed experimentation and innovation with approaches such as scorecards, social audits, and use of new information technologies to facilitate social monitoring, as well as operational and analytical work at the World Bank.

Citizens and Service Delivery: Assessing the Use of Social Accountability Approaches in the Human Development Sectors looks at the use of social accountability in the human development sectors—health, education, and social protection. Perhaps more than other public services, these services involve frequent contacts between citizens and providers. The quality of the interactions, for example, between students and teachers, doctors and patients, and vulnerable households and social workers can influence the outcomes of services and shape citizens' relations with their governments in a direct way. In theory, if citizens have access to information about their rights and the type and quality of services that they should expect, and if they have opportunities to use this information to affect the behavior of providers and the decisions of policy makers, they can influence service delivery.

This book looks at how this works in practice. It aims to learn from the experiences gained from the implementation of World Bank projects and from the small, but growing, set of impact evaluations. The review is a first step to identify lessons, knowledge gaps, and questions for further research that can improve the use of these tools in government policies and through programs supported by civil society and donors, including the World Bank.

The book documents a diverse and exciting set of cases—the rapid adoption of access-to-information laws, the use of public expenditure tracking surveys by civil society organizations to "follow the money" from central government budgets to schools and health clinics, and the incorporation of grievance redress mechanisms into the design of conditional cash transfer programs.

Many of the examples discussed here are new initiatives, and some are being evaluated now. Much will be gained from more evaluation and the sharing of experiences across countries—developed and developing alike.

Ariel Fiszbein
Chief Economist, Human Development Network
World Bank

About the Authors

Dena Ringold is a Senior Economist in the Human Development Network, Office of the Chief Economist at the World Bank. Her research interests include governance, service delivery, and inclusion of minorities. Prior to joining the Chief Economist's Office, she worked in the Europe and Central Asia Region and the Latin America and the Caribbean Region at the World Bank.

Alaka Holla is an Economist in the Human Development Network, Office of the Chief Economist. Her area of research focuses on measuring the quality of service delivery; the demand for quality; and the relationships among prices, access, and quality in health and education markets. She holds a Ph.D. in Economics from Brown University.

Margaret Koziol is a Policy Adviser and Education Officer at the United States Agency for International Development. Her work focuses on using evaluation to improve education programming, improving early grade reading results, and producing research related to service delivery and governance, particularly in conflict and fragile environments. Formerly, she worked as a consultant in the Human Development Network, Office of the Chief Economist, where her work focused on governance and service delivery in human development.

Santhosh Srinivasan is a Consultant in the Human Development Network, Office of the Chief Economist. His research interests include governance and service delivery. Prior to joining the Human Development Network, he worked for the Development Economics Finance and Private Sector Development Group, where he oversaw field implementation of randomized impact evaluation studies.

Acknowledgments

This volume was prepared by a team in the Office of the Chief Economist for Human Development at the World Bank, led by Dena Ringold and including Alaka Holla, Margaret Koziol, and Santhosh Srinivasan. Ariel Fiszbein, Chief Economist, provided guidance to the team. The book draws from background papers by Varun Gauri, World Bank (grievance redress mechanisms); Chris van Stolk, RAND UK (grievance redress in Organisation for Economic Co-operation and Development countries); and Richard Calland and Kristina Bentley, University of Cape Town, South Africa (access to information). Silke Hauser provided assistance with the review of project documents.

The book also draws from interviews and written surveys with a large number of Human Development staff and incorporates materials from project case studies, including "Brazil, Bolsa Familia": Anna Fruttero, Catalina Gomez, and Dena Ringold; "Peru, RECURSO": Ian Walker and Carmen Osorio; "Indonesia, BOS-KITA": Rivandra Royono; "Madagascar, Health Scorecards": Sarah Keener, Andrianjaka Razafimandimby, and Margaret Koziol; and "Cambodia, Education": Omporn Regel and Margaret Koziol.

Peer reviewers were Yamini Aiyar (Accountability Initiative); Robert Chase (World Bank); Polly Jones (World Bank); Andrew Norton (ODI); Courtney Tolmie (TAP/Results for Development); and Abdo Yazbeck (World Bank). Comments and useful guidance were also received from Carine Clert, Tommaso Balbo di Vinadio, Helene Grandvoinnet, Charles Griffin, Sina Odugbemi, Mario Picon, Ritva Reinikka, and Shekhar Shah.

Abbreviations

ATI	access to information
BOS	School Operational Grant
CBPS	Centre for Budget and Policy Studies (India)
CCT	conditional cash transfer
CIEN	Centro de Investigaciones Económicas Nacionales (Guatemala)
CRAS	Centros de Referencia de Assistencia Social (Brazil)
CSO	civil society organization
DFGG	demand for good governance
DPL	development policy loan
EBRD	European Bank for Reconstruction and Development
FTA	financial transparency and accountability
FY	fiscal year
GAC	governance and anticorruption (strategy)
GRM	grievance redress mechanisms
HD	human development
HEPS	Health Promotion and Social Development (Uganda)
HNP	health, nutrition, and population
HSNP	Hunger Safety Net Programme (Kenya)
IFAI	Instituto Federal de Acceso a la Información Pública (Mexico)

IPAR	Institute of Policy Analysis and Research
MASAF	Malawi Social Action Fund
MDS	Ministry of Social Development
MP	Madhya Pradesh, India
NAO	National Audit Office (United Kingdom)
NGO	nongovernmental organization
NREGA	National Rural Employment Guarantee Act (India)
OECD	Organisation for Economic Co-operation and Development
PAD	project appraisal document
PBS	Protection of Basic Services (project) (Ethiopia)
PDS	Public Distribution System (India)
PETS	public expenditure tracking survey
POS	Plan Obligatorio de Salud (Colombia)
POSS	Plan Obligatorio de Salud Subsidiado (Colombia)
RECURSO	Rendición de Cuentas para la Reforma Social (Peru)
RTIA	Right to Information Act (India)
SP	social protection
TAC	Treatment Action Campaign (South Africa)
TAP	Transparency and Accountability Program
TI	Transparency International
UP	Uttar Pradesh, India
VEC	village education committee
WDR	*World Development Report*

CHAPTER 1

Introduction and Conceptual Framework

In many low- and middle-income countries, dismal failures in the quality of public service delivery are demonstrated by high rates of absenteeism among teachers and doctors; leakages of public funds intended for schools, health clinics, or social assistance benefits; and shortages and stock-outs of pharmaceuticals and textbooks. These failures have driven the agenda for better governance and accountability. Governments, civil society, and donors have become increasingly interested in the idea that citizens can contribute to improved quality of service delivery by holding policy makers and providers of services accountable. This proposition is particularly resonant when it comes to the human development (HD) sectors—health, education, and social protection—which involve close interactions between providers and the citizens who use their services.

This idea has been shaped by the influential *2004 World Development Report: Making Services Work for Poor People* (World Bank 2003). The *WDR* defined a framework for analyzing accountability relationships among policy makers, providers, and citizens. Within this framework, accountability can be implemented through either a "long route," whereby citizens influence policy makers who in turn influence service delivery through providers, or a "short route," through which citizens—

individually and collectively—can directly influence, participate in, and supervise service delivery by providers.

Donors, governments, and nongovernmental organizations (NGOs) have been experimenting with various social accountability tools that aim to inform citizens and communities about their rights, the standards of service delivery they should expect, and actual performance. They also aim to facilitate access to formal redress mechanisms to deal with service failures. But what is known about how these approaches actually work in practice? Can giving people information and opportunities to use that information actually improve service delivery? And what are the implications for development agencies such as the World Bank? The objective of this book is to explore what is currently known about the opportunities and limitations of these types of social accountability approaches in the HD sectors.

The book reviews how citizens, individually and collectively, can influence service delivery through access to information and through the opportunities to use it to hold providers—both frontline service providers and program managers—accountable. The book takes stock of what is known from international evidence and from projects supported by the World Bank to identify knowledge gaps, key questions, and areas for further work. It aims to synthesize experience to date, identify what resources are needed to support more effective use of social accountability tools and approaches, and formulate considerations for their use in human development.

This chapter discusses the conceptual framework and rationale for this review and clarifies concepts and terms. Chapter 2 presents a review of how World Bank projects in HD are incorporating social accountability, based on a portfolio analysis and surveys of staff in the sector. Chapter 3 discusses experience with information interventions, and chapter 4 examines redress of grievances. The final chapter offers some considerations for future efforts to use social accountability to improve service delivery in the HD sectors.

Rationale: Why Focus on This Topic?

There are a number of reasons to address this topic. Within the development community, interest in the potential for citizens to hold service providers accountable is closely linked with an increased focus on governance and its role in achieving better service delivery. While not a new phenomenon, social accountability approaches have been receiving greater consideration as a path to strengthen governance and accountability. "Demand for good governance" (DFGG), for example, is a core focus of the World Bank's Governance and Anticorruption (GAC) strategy.[1]

This push to mainstream governance in country programs and development projects is showing up in HD programs, including those financed by the World Bank. In response to recent financial crises, the rapid growth of cash transfer programs in the social protection sector has lent increased importance to establishing credible mechanisms for auditing payments and targeting beneficiaries to reduce risks of error, fraud, and corruption (van Stolk and Tesliuc 2010; Khan and Giannozzi 2011). At least eight health projects in the World Bank's portfolio are experimenting with scorecards to improve accountability of service delivery.

A related development has been the recognition that civil society organizations (CSOs) can be important in the delivery of social services and in social accountability. Their participation may include initiating campaigns to inform citizens about their rights and what services they are entitled to, performing third-party monitoring through processes such as social audits, and conducting analyses. They may undertake analysis such as public expenditure tracking surveys (PETS) to "follow the money" from central government budgets through to service providers, or absenteeism surveys to monitor attendance of providers (Koziol and Tolmie 2010; Rogers and Koziol 2011).

The growing pressure to focus on results on the ground in development projects reinforces the importance of improving monitoring and evaluation systems, particularly in contexts of weak accountability. An example is the adoption of results-based approaches through which funds are disbursed according to the achievement of measurable results. World Bank–financed health projects in countries from Argentina to Zambia are linking disbursements to service delivery results, such as the number of children vaccinated or women receiving prenatal care.[2] These approaches often call for a stronger role for citizens in monitoring and evaluation to ensure that results are achieved.

Governments and civil society organizations alike have a growing interest in the potential for information and communication technology to serve as a tool for strengthening service delivery accountability. The wide coverage of mobile phones has been particularly influential in motivating new applications of mobile technology. Various innovations are emerging in the HD sectors and are being built into management information systems. Examples include the use of mobile phones to report pharmaceutical stock-outs, websites for posting local school budgets, and grievance redress mechanisms for reporting problems in conditional cash transfer (CCT) programs.

This book builds on and complements recent related reviews and analyses that looked at issues related to social accountability and the demand side of governance in human development. One example is a World Bank book on school accountability, *Making Schools Work: New Evidence on Accountability Reforms* (Bruns, Filmer, and Patrinos 2011). The book synthesizes impact evaluations of accountability reforms related to information, school-based management, and teacher policies. The World Bank and other partners have also conducted a number of recent reviews and stocktakings of governance and social accountability in HD and other sectors.[3]

Governance and Service Delivery: A Conceptual Framework

From the perspective of service delivery, governance can be understood as the set of incentives, accountability arrangements, and rules that affect the way key actors—including policy makers and provider organizations and their managers and staff—are held accountable for their behaviors and ability to deliver high-quality services with efficiency and responsiveness. In this regard, governance can be seen as a set of principal-agent relations that are defined by the incentives facing each of the agents and the accountability mechanisms that are available to the principals.

In this discussion, the term *policy makers* refers to the high-level elected officials or civil servants responsible for carrying out legislative and regulatory responsibilities, and *providers* are the program managers, local officials, and others involved in the administration and delivery of services, as well as frontline providers, such as doctors, teachers, and social workers, who interact directly with the public.

The accountability framework of the 2004 *WDR* is a useful starting point for identifying the entry points for influencing the quality, efficiency, and responsiveness of service delivery. The main channels for strengthening accountability are the institutions and relationships between the three sets of actors: policy makers and politicians, service providers, and citizens (figure 1.1).

First, the **compact** between politicians and providers depends on the quality of the institutions, rules, regulations, and incentive arrangements made through channels such as intergovernmental institutional relations, civil service and human resource policies, budget planning and execution, public financial management, transparency and information mechanisms, regulatory systems, monitoring and evaluation, and formal controls, such as external audits.

Figure 1.1   Accountability Relationships in Service Delivery

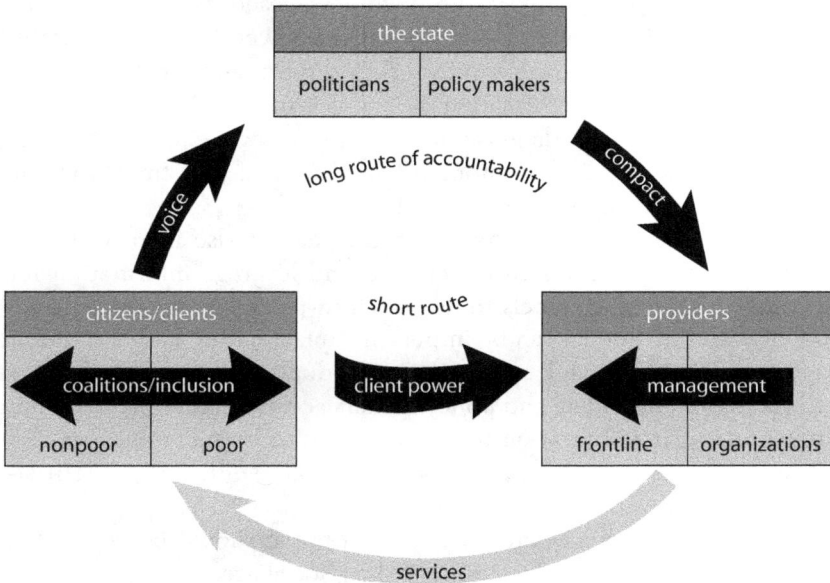

Source: World Bank 2003.

Second, the interaction of citizens and policy makers takes place through channels for expressing **voice**, including votes, taxes, and representation in parliament and other political bodies. Voice can be facilitated by making information available to citizens, through national-level legal frameworks providing for access to information and by more micro-level tools such as report cards, which provide people with information about how services they use are performing. Grievance redress mechanisms, which are discussed in this book, can also be channels for voice—if complaints and feedback are aggregated to influence policy.

Third, **client power** refers to the direct influence that citizens can have on service providers. Citizens can exert influence through participation in service delivery, perhaps by assuming some responsibility for delivery, contracting, or involvement in the governance of provision—for example, by joining parent-teacher associations. Choice is an important way citizens can express their client power—although it is often overlooked as an expression of accountability. Client power can also be exercised through the types of social accountability mechanisms discussed in this book, including interventions that equip people with information about their rights and services and grievance redress mechanisms.

Citizens and users of services can affect social services by influencing the decisions of policy makers—through voice—and by influencing the behavior of service providers—through client power. To exert this influence, they need *access to information* about services and the *capacity* and *opportunities* to use the information and transform it into action. Increasing transparency and providing access to information require efforts to improve the availability of information, as well as investments in the quality, relevance, and timeliness of information.

Expanding opportunities for using information also involves building the capacity of users to understand and leverage information for action and opening channels to use it. Third-party intermediaries such as CSOs and the media can be important to facilitating access to information and redress and translating individual efforts into collective efforts to hold providers and policy makers accountable.[4] The idea that citizens can use information to secure access to better services is also consistent with rights-based approaches to service delivery (Gacitúa-Marió, Norton, and Georgieva 2009).

The emphasis here is on citizen action, but it should be noted that action by policy makers is critical to making social accountability mechanisms work. Policy makers create the incentives and processes for ensuring that individual and institutional providers adapt their behavior and performance in response to citizens' demands. For example, policy makers are responsible for setting the framework for providers to respond to access-to-information requests or to change performance in response to complaints. Chile's AUGE health reform plan explicitly clarified the state's intent to be held accountable for service delivery through a guarantee of service standards (Gacitúa-Marió, Norton, and Georgieva 2009).

Although voting, choice, and participation in service delivery are potentially important channels for improving accountability, they are not the focus of this book. Instead, the focus is on two related categories of social accountability interventions that are increasingly being incorporated into government programs and World Bank support: information interventions and grievance redress mechanisms. Both involve efforts to inform citizens and provide them with opportunities to use information and influence service delivery.

Social Accountability Terms and Tools

Odugbemi and Lee (2011) note that international development institutions have become enamored with accountability, but they point out the risk that it has become a buzzword: "At the time of writing, actors in development appear to delight in announcing their intention to 'promote accountability' far more often than they know what it means to do so." Associated with this phenomenon is a proliferation of terms around accountability—*social accountability, empowerment, demand for good governance, and demand-side governance,* among others—which can cause confusion. This section discusses the terms and tools that are used in this book.

In the context of service delivery, accountability can be exerted top-down from higher-level officials; sideways through competition or peer pressure from other providers; externally by international and multilateral organizations, other states, and outside actors; and bottom-up by citizens, CSOs, NGOs, and the media (Griffin et al. 2010).

Social accountability is another term for bottom-up accountability. In this book, social accountability refers to the set of tools that citizens can use to influence the quality of service delivery by holding providers accountable (box 1.1; table 1.1). The book focuses on the set of interventions that aims to inform citizens, individually and collectively, about their rights, the services and benefits they are entitled to receive, the performance standards they should expect, and the grievance redress channels they can use when things go wrong.

In practice, the distinction between information campaigns and grievance redress mechanisms is not as sharply drawn as this discussion may suggest. Grievance redress mechanisms may also disseminate information—for example, a hotline for a CCT program that collects complaints and responds to queries about benefit eligibility criteria and payment amounts.

References to social accountability as demand-side interventions can be misleading, as they require cooperation with the supply side at various levels of government. For example, scorecards require effective interactions between citizens and frontline service providers and program managers. These officials need incentives and capacity to respond to citizens. Civil society actors also have key roles in the implementation of social accountability interventions in helping make information available and accessible. They can gather data for a PETS, deliver training on budget literacy, and help citizens file complaints and access redress mechanisms.

Information Interventions

If they want to influence service provision, citizens would ideally have two tools: access to information and the opportunity to use the information

Box 1.1

A Note about Terminology

The development discourse and literature use various terms that relate to the ideas discussed in this box: that informing citizens about their rights and quality standards and providing opportunities to use information through grievance redress can lead to better service delivery outcomes. We use the following terms in the text:

Social accountability interventions refer to efforts to provide information to citizens and channels to enable them to use the information to hold service providers accountable. They refer to efforts to increase the *agency* of citizens, both individually and collectively, through CSOs and other intermediaries.

The book discusses two sets of social accountability mechanisms: first, *information interventions*, which involve project and policy measures ranging from simple information provision, such as right-to-information legislation, information campaigns, and report cards, to more active steps, such as scorecards and social audits, that engage citizens to use information to influence providers; and, second, *grievance redress mechanisms*, also known as *complaints-handling mechanisms*, which are formal channels for citizens to demand their rights, complain, and provide feedback to providers and policy makers about service delivery.

Social accountability interventions are a subset of the broader set of *demand-side* governance activities that includes community-driven development and participation in the management and delivery of services (such as participatory budgeting and school-based management), which are outside the scope of this book. The World Bank's GAC strategy refers to this set of tools, which relate to transparency, accountability, and participation as *demand for good governance*.

The book uses the terms *citizens, recipients, consumers,* and *users* of services interchangeably to refer to the people who are supposed to receive and benefit from health, education, and social protection programs and services. None of these terms is ideal: referring to *citizens* potentially excludes noncitizens—for example, refugees and unregistered populations—who may be eligible for services or benefits and have valid roles to play in influencing the delivery of services, and the terms *recipients* and *users* suggest that people actually receive services and benefits even when they may not.

Source: Authors.

Table 1.1   Examples of Social Accountability Interventions

Information interventions	
Access-to-information legislation	A legal framework for public provision of information.
Information campaigns	Efforts to inform citizens about their rights to services, quality standards, and performance.
Report cards	A type of information campaign that provides information about service performance to citizens, sometimes in the form of a ranking of providers. Some report cards may include facilitated discussions with citizens.
Scorecards	A quantitative survey of citizen satisfaction with public services that includes a facilitated meeting between providers and beneficiaries to discuss results and agree on follow-up actions.
Social audits	A participatory audit in which community members compare stated expenditures or services delivered with actual outputs.
Grievance redress mechanisms	
Redress in line ministries	Various venues established at the policy, program, and project levels for collecting feedback, grievances, and complaints.
Independent redress institutions	Structures outside government agencies, including tribunals, ombudsmen, public inquiries, civil society organizations, and a variety of sector-specific entities such as labor relations boards.
Courts	Legal redress mechanisms through the court system.

Source: Authors.

and transform it into action. The category of social accountability measures referred to here as *information interventions* focuses on the first step: informing people. In addition, some types of interventions—for example, scorecards—incorporate more active elements, such as feedback sessions with providers that give people venues to use information for influencing service providers. Examples and experience with these types of information interventions are discussed in more detail in chapter 3.

Access-to-information legislation. The political and institutional context for access to information is shaped by the existence of formal rules, institutional channels, and provisions for informing citizens about their rights. Access to information is a right in a growing number of countries. Approximately 50 countries have specified access to information in their constitutions, and 80 countries have passed self-standing access-to-information laws.

Information campaigns. The term *information campaign* describes a broad category of efforts to educate the public and can cover any number of topics—from marketing products to encouraging people not to smoke. This book discusses those campaigns that aim to encourage accountability by informing people about public services, including what services they are entitled to receive, how to access them, and about their performance and quality. This kind of information campaign implicitly encourages citizens to demand better services by publicizing information about rights, standards, and performance. Information campaigns in the HD sectors are important mechanisms to stimulate demand for services or to change behavior—for example, a hand-washing campaign. Such campaigns are, however, outside the scope of this book.

Information campaigns can range from passive provision of information to more active efforts to engage citizens. On the more passive end of the spectrum, **report cards** refer to a type of information campaign that provides comparative information on services.[5] In Organisation for Economic Co-operation Development (OECD) countries, report cards have been utilized as an accountability mechanism primarily for health service delivery. They usually combine a beneficiary satisfaction survey with objective indicators used to benchmark facilities against one another.

Scorecards and social audits are more active information interventions that involve face-to-face interactions between citizens and providers. They also facilitate collective action of users of services vis-à-vis providers. **Scorecards** are based on a quantitative survey of service users that assesses their satisfaction and experiences with various dimensions of service delivery. They also involve an additional step: a discussion between the recipients of services (for example, patients at a health clinic or parents of schoolchildren) and service providers (doctors, teachers, and facility managers) to discuss the findings of the survey and to develop a follow-up plan.

The **social audit** is a form of community monitoring that allows citizens who receive a service to review and cross-check the information reported by the service provider against information collected from users of the service. This form of monitoring could review various aspects of the service delivery process such as whether allocated funds actually reached the health facility, whether people who met eligibility criteria receive social assistance benefits, and whether providers show up for work. The results of the audit are usually announced during public gatherings, which are generally attended by users as well as public officials involved in management of services and providers. India's National Rural Employment Guarantee Scheme, for example, incorporates an active program of social audits.

Grievance Redress Mechanisms

Grievance redress mechanisms (GRMs) provide people with opportunities to use information to influence service delivery. They are formal accountability mechanisms for citizens to give feedback on government programs and services when problems arise. They are generally the accountability channel of last resort for complaints that are not resolved at the point of delivery. Most grievance redress mechanisms allow individuals to give feedback about services, such as a parent registering a complaint about teacher conduct or conditions at a school. When feedback is aggregated, however, it can be used to influence provision at the program or policy level. Chapter 4 discusses experience with grievance redress mechanisms.

Grievance redress mechanisms can be categorized into three main types: redress within government agencies; independent redress institutions, such as ombudsmen and CSOs; and courts. The three types can be briefly defined as follows:

Redress within government agencies. Government agencies can establish a variety of venues for receiving complaints and grievances at the policy, program, and project levels, including dedicated mailboxes, e-mail addresses, text messaging systems, telephone hotlines, interactive websites, office windows, and complaints-handling officers. These sites can be inside service provision points, such as hospitals or schools, or in separate offices within the ministries. They can be specialized offices, focusing on a particular kind of problem, such as not receiving a cash transfer, or they can be open to any kind of comment or complaint. One form of specialized venue is the project-related complaints-handling procedure, which may focus exclusively on donor-funded activities.

Independent redress institutions. Another category of redress mechanisms includes tribunals, ombudsmen, public inquiries, CSOs, and a variety of sector-specific entities, such as labor relations boards. These mechanisms are distinguished from redress mechanisms within government agencies in that they sit outside of the formal government bureaucracy and sometimes possess little or no public authority to compel parties to accept their findings. Their role, especially that of ombudsmen, can be to enforce compliance within an overall legal and policy framework.

Courts. Depending on local legal traditions, institutional configurations, and political circumstances, courts can hear and redress the failures of line agencies and providers to comply with their statutory and contractual obligations. Courts can review the regulations that govern service delivery in light of prevailing laws.

Why Should These Instruments Work?

Why would social accountability measures that aim to inform citizens and provide opportunities for redress be expected to improve the quality of service delivery? What is the causal theory of change implicit in the design of these interventions? It is useful to step back and review why and how these approaches are expected to strengthen service delivery in the HD sectors and what evidence exists to support these assumptions.

A literature review of impact evaluations in the HD sectors found a limited number of studies that empirically test whether providing information to citizens has an effect on service delivery or HD outcomes.[6] No empirical evaluations of grievance redress mechanisms were found. The majority of the evaluations were conducted in South Asia and East Africa. Although it is too early to draw firm conclusions from this limited set of experiments, and although they cover only a subset of what is being implemented in practice, the findings are useful in pointing to implications for further research and operational work.

Assumptions along the Accountability Chain

The 2004 *WDR* framework hypothesizes that equipping citizens with information and redress mechanisms can improve the quality of service delivery. Implicit in both the short and the long routes of accountability are a number of assumptions. First, on the citizen side, the framework assumes that people have the ability and incentives to access and process information about service delivery. Second, it assumes that—if opportunities exist—people are willing and able to use information and redress channels to put pressure on policy makers and providers. Finally, the framework assumes that policy makers and providers will be responsive to citizen influence.

Evidence from the political science literature indicates that citizens do use information in making voting decisions. Citizens are the principals, and politicians are their agents who are supposed to deliver public services on their behalf, and information about politicians' performance allows voters to reward or punish politicians during elections (Besley and Preston 2007). There is ample empirical evidence from impact evaluations in low- and middle-income countries showing that voters take such information into account (Pande 2011). Greater newspaper penetration rates in India, for example, improved government responsiveness to droughts and floods (Besley and Burgess 2002), just as radio stations strengthened the impact of expenditure audits on an incumbent's chances of reelection during municipal elections in Brazil (Ferraz and Finan 2008).

Does a similar logic transfer to service providers, who are not elected and typically not hired, fired, or paid on the basis of their performance? Information campaigns can expose corruption or inform people about the relative merits of choosing one provider over another, and redress mechanisms can give people channels to give feedback, but do such interventions automatically enable or empower people to demand better services from their existing providers? If redress mechanisms are available, will people use them? And will they work?

Can Citizens Hold Providers Accountable?
Relationships between providers and individual citizens are complex and may not change easily or quickly. Citizens may not be willing or able to challenge providers if they lack information or time or if they do not feel empowered to do so. The latter is particularly salient in low-income countries, where providers may come from more affluent backgrounds and citizens may not feel in a position to question them. People may not think that they have the right or authority to challenge a teacher or doctor because of their status, credentials, or knowledge, or they may be concerned about the repercussions of giving negative feedback.

A recent survey in rural Madhya Pradesh, India, included direct observations in clinics and found that the median patient asked zero questions during an interaction with his or her provider.[7] Similarly, in rural Mexico, focus groups assessing school-based management found that indigenous groups and the poor were unlikely to question school leadership (Bruns, Filmer, and Patrinos 2011).

Lack of information limits the extent to which citizens interact with providers. A nationally representative school survey in Albania suggests that 25 percent of parents did not know the name of their child's mathematics teacher, and more than 40 percent were not aware of the existence of a school board with parent representatives in their school (Serra, Barr, and Packard 2011). In rural Uttar Pradesh, the relationship between schools and parents is weaker than in Albania: only 7 percent of parents knew about their village education committee (VEC), and less than 15 percent of parents had complained about their school.

In the HD sectors, asymmetric information can limit the extent to which citizens are able to challenge policy makers and providers. Sufficient knowledge about disease causation or the efficacy of preventive health services often comes only with advanced education or medical training. If test scores or other markers of school performance are not publicly available, parents—especially less educated parents—may find it difficult to assess school quality. There is a also a risk that limited knowledge about appropriate inputs could undermine the quality of services if people decide that good teachers are their cousins or good doctors always give injections.

Citizens may have difficulties in establishing a causal relationship between providers' actions and final outcomes, such as test scores or health status. In India, 75 percent of parents thought that parents bear the most responsibility for school quality (Banerjee et al. 2010). Qualitative evidence from India also points to the challenge of learning through observation about the link between disease susceptibility and immunization status even after an epidemic. Vaccinated children tend to live in better homes and are more likely to wear shoes, and therefore it is easy to see why parents have a difficult time attributing disease immunity to vaccination or the actions of health care providers (Das and Das 2003).

Another constraint may be time and attention span. Citizens, and particularly the poor, simply may not have the time to get informed or give feedback on service delivery through grievance redress mechanisms. Social accountability interventions that involve citizens can take time. In a field experiment with community targeting of a cash transfer program in Indonesia, villagers ranked everyone in the village from richest to poorest according to their wealth. The meetings ran longer than one and one-half hours and involved ranking 54 households, which no doubt required a high degree of sustained attention (Alatas et al. 2011).

In one experiment, the order in which these households were presented to villagers was randomized. For households presented earlier in the meeting, the villagers' rankings were relatively accurate at identifying the poor, but the community-based targeting worsened as the meeting progressed (Alatas et al. 2011), which suggests that fatigue might have set in and undermined the value of including the community in targeting decisions. Such results suggest that program managers may be burdening citizens when they ask them to track budget allocations for their local schools or clinics or devise a plan for improving services in their area. Members of poor households may not have time for participation in local governance because of more pressing priorities such as securing food and meeting other basic needs (Banerjee and Mullainathan 2008).

Further evidence that people are preoccupied with more immediate needs and may not have the attention span to properly monitor providers comes from village meetings in India in which parents were encouraged to question village education committees and local government officials about education (Banerjee et al. 2010). Parents were most animated about scholarships they felt their children should be getting and about a midday meal program, and facilitators of the meetings struggled to focus the discussions on broader issues of learning (Khemani 2007).

Thus, it should not be surprising when mobilization efforts run out of steam once an intervention ends. When parents in Kenya were trained to monitor the activities of contract teachers in their schools and hold performance reviews, test scores improved in one year. This learning advantage disappeared, however, one year after the contract teacher program ended (Duflo, Dupas, and Kremer 2010), suggesting that parents may not have maintained their monitoring activities. Unfortunately, it is impossible to gauge the extent to which the problem with sustainability can be generalized because so few evaluations collect follow-up data more than one year after an intervention. It is therefore not possible to know if these interventions generate merely a momentary blip in behavior or if they have the potential to permanently alter client-provider relations for the better.

Finally, people may not act on information for accountability if they lack an immediate action plan or tool. Insights from behavioral economics support this point. In an experiment with an information campaign for tetanus immunizations at Yale University, some students received a specific plan that showed on a map the health center where students could be vaccinated, listed its hours of operation and where exactly students should go, and requested students to choose a time for going to the health center. Actual rates of inoculation increased only for those who received a specific action plan, even though the students who read a fear-inducing message did express a higher intention to get a shot (Leventhal, Singer, and Jones 1965).

The need for an immediate action plan to be coupled with information provision may also affect major investment decisions, such as the choice to go to college. Experiments with a national tax-filing service provider in the United States showed that some basic help with filling out financial aid forms had a sizable impact on financial aid receipt and college atten-dance among low- and middle-income households (Bettinger et al. 2009). Aid receipt and college attendance rates did not budge for tax filers who received calculations of their aid eligibility, information about tuition prices, and encouragement to fill out a financial aid form. Another set of filers received the same information, but their tax information was also used to fill in some parts of the financial aid application in advance. A 10-minute interview elicited the rest of the required information, and the tax-filing service provider then mailed in the application forms. As a result, this group received more financial aid, and their college attendance rate increased by 26 percent.

Parents in India also responded more often when offered a specific tool to address learning shortfalls that they could put into action immediately. When information about the poor quality of learning in public schools was coupled with training for organizing reading camps, each village held multiple camps and children's literacy improved (Banerjee et al. 2010).

Do Providers Respond to Citizen Influence?

When citizens use information for accountability, do providers respond? Some of the existing experimental and quasi-experimental evidence sug-gests that information campaigns can be effective in improving providers' accountability to their clients.

A small experiment in China suggests that patients acting on information—in particular, questioning whether a certain medical treat-ment is necessary—affects how providers treat them. When an incognito standardized patient presenting with symptoms of a cold mentioned that he or she had read that antibiotics were not appropriate for simple colds, health care providers were 25 percentage points less likely to prescribe antibiotics (Currie, Lin, and Zhang 2010). Although this result suggests that drug overprescription and the consequent expenditure burden on patients can be reduced when patients actively signal what they know, it is also important to note that the standardized patients who questioned their providers also observed lower levels of respect and care.

Some of the interventions that are discussed in chapter 3 provide insights on this matter. A school report card experiment in Pakistan seemed to change the relationship between providers and their clients. Test scores improved in both public schools and private schools after the distribution of a report card that listed a school's performance relative to other schools in the area and a child's relative performance in his or her school. Three trends suggest that these learning improvements stemmed from an increase in provider accountability rather than parents switching to a better school. First, schools increased their investment in inputs and the length of the school day, while investments by households changed very little. Second, after the intervention fewer parents switched schools. Third, schools that had little room to improve school quality reduced the fees they charged (and therefore the economic rents that they earned) when parents learned of their relative standing in the community (Andrabi, Das, and Khwaja 2009).

In other studies, however, the relationship between providers and clients did not change at all. Instead, the information campaigns most likely stimulated demand for services that were not being used. An information campaign in India informed people of their rights to free services in public health clinics, and evidence from a randomized evaluation suggests that the take-up of certain entitled services increased dramatically, but only for services that involved beneficiaries coming to the clinics. The intervention showed no significant impact on services that required service providers to leave their clinics, nor did target beneficiaries increase their participation in local politics (Pandey et al. 2007). In a quasi-experiment in Benin, children's literacy increased in villages that received more radio signals from community stations, which exposed more people to education- and health-related programming. The intervention had no significant impact on public investment in schools or households' knowledge of education-related policies of the government (Keefer and Khemani 2011).

This discussion of accountability relationships between citizens and providers raises a number of points. First, interactions between providers and citizens take place in a context of social, political, historical, and cultural dynamics that may not change easily or quickly. Second, it is difficult to distinguish when increased access to information merely serves as a stimulus to the demand for services from changes to provider behavior. Some citizens may not know about the availability or relative quality of services or may have never contemplated the potential benefits of those services, but when they become informed, they may change their behavior either by increasing their utilization or by switching providers.[8] Third, information interventions and grievance redress mechanisms may not improve the quality of service delivery on their own, which implies that the broader setting for these interactions deserves consideration, including the political and legal context for access to information and redress; the roles of and incentives faced by policy makers, civil society, and other

actors involved in service delivery; and the design of the social accountability mechanisms themselves. These issues are discussed in chapters 3
and 4.

Notes

1. Resources on the World Bank's work on governance, including implementation of the GAC strategy, can be found at http://www.worldbank.org/
   governance.
2. See http://www.rbfhealth.org/rbfhealth/.
3. Two examples are a review of DFGG at the World Bank by the Partnership for
   Transparency Fund, http://ptfund.org/special-projects/ptf-report-stimulating-
   demand-for-good-governance/, and a multidonor review financed by the U.K.
   Department of International Development. A summary of this work is available
   at http://www.transparency-initiative.org/reports/synthesis-report-impact-and-
   effectiveness-of-transparency-and-accountability-initiatives.
4. See Odugbemi and Lee (2011) for further discussion of the links between
   accountability, public opinion, and collective action.
5. Report cards are sometimes confused with citizen report cards, which are a
   methodology for a quantitative survey of citizen satisfaction with public services similar to scorecards. This book refers to report cards as a type of information campaign that provides information about performance of services to
   citizens.
6. These studies are summarized in appendix 2.
7. Based on Das and Das's (2003) initial analyses of data from an ongoing project in India.
8. Additional methodological challenges of evaluating accountability interventions are discussed in more detail in appendix 1.

References

Alatas, Vivi, Abhijit Banerjee, Rema Hanna, Benjamin A. Olken, and Julia Tobias.
2011. "Targeting the Poor: Evidence from a Field Experiment in Indonesia."
Working Paper 15980, National Bureau of Economic Research, Cambridge,
MA. http://www.nber.org/papers/w15980.pdf.

Andrabi, Tahir, Jishnu Das, and Asim Ijaz Khwaja. 2009. "Report Cards: The
Impact of Providing School and Child Test-Scores on Educational Markets."
Unpublished manuscript, Department of Economics, Harvard University.
http://www.hks.harvard.edu/fs/akhwaja/papers/RC_08Oct09Full.pdf.

Banerjee, Abhijit V., Rukmini Banerji, Esther Duflo, Rachel Glennerster, and Stuti
Khemani. 2010. "Pitfalls in Participatory Programs: Evidence from a Randomized

Evaluation in Education in India." *American Economic Journal: Economic Policy* 2 (1): 1–30. http://pubs.aeaweb.org/doi/pdfplus/10.1257/pol.2.1.1.

Banerjee, Abhijit V., and Sendhil Mullainathan. 2008. "Limited Attention and Income Distribution." Unpublished manuscript, Department of Economics, Harvard University. http://www.economics.harvard.edu/faculty/mullainathan/files/CoverPage.AEA.Jan04_2008.session.pdf.

Besley, Timothy, and Robin Burgess. 2002. "The Political Economy of Government Responsiveness: Theory and Evidence from India." Discussion Paper 2721, Centre for Economic Policy Research, London. http://sticerd.lse.ac.uk/dps/de/dedps28a.pdf.

Besley, Timothy, and Ian Preston. 2007. "Electoral Bias and Policy Choice: Theory and Evidence." *Quarterly Journal of Economics* 122 (4): 1473–510. http://qje.oxfordjournals.org/content/122/4/1473.full.pdf+html.

Bettinger, Eric P., Bridget Terry Long, Philip Oreopoulos, and Lisa Sanbonmatsu. 2009. "The Role of Simplification and Information in College Decisions: Results from the H&R Block FAFSA Experiment." Working Paper 15361, National Bureau of Economic Research, Cambridge, MA. http://www.nber.org/papers/w15361.pdf?new_window=1.

Bruns, Barbara, Deon Filmer, and Harry Anthony Patrinos. 2011. *Making Schools Work: New Evidence on Accountability Reforms.* Washington, DC: World Bank. http://siteresources.worldbank.org/EDUCATION/Resources/278200-1298568319076/makingschoolswork.pdf.

Currie, Janet, Wanchuan Lin, and Wei Zhang. 2010. "Patient Knowledge and Antibiotic Abuse: Evidence from an Audit Study in China." Working Paper 16602, National Bureau of Economic Research, Cambridge, MA. http://www.nber.org/papers/w16602.pdf.

Das, Jishnu, and Saumya Das. 2003. "Trust, Learning, and Vaccination: A Case Study of a North Indian Village." *Social Science and Medicine* 57: 97–112. http://www.sciencedirect.com/science/article/pii/S0277953602003027.

Duflo, Esther, Pascaline Dupas, and Michael Kremer. 2010. "Additional Resources versus Organizational Changes in Education: Experimental Evidence from Kenya." Unpublished manuscript, Department of Economics, Massachusetts Institute of Technology. http://econ-www.mit.edu/files/4286.

Ferraz, Claudio, and Frederico Finan. 2008. "Exposing Corrupt Politicians: The Effects of Brazil's Publicly Released Audits on Electoral Outcomes." *Quarterly Journal of Economics* 123 (2): 703–45. http://qje.oxfordjournals.org/content/123/2/703.full.pdf+html.

Gacitúa-Marió, Estanislao, Andrew Norton, and Sophia V. Georgieva, eds. 2009. *Building Equality and Opportunity through Social Guarantees: New Approaches to Public Policy and the Realization of Rights.* Washington, DC: World Bank. http://www.fundacionpobreza.cl/descarga-archivo/building_equality.pdf.

Griffin, Charles, David de Ferranti, Courtney Tolmie, Justin Jacinto, Graeme Ramshaw, and Chinyere Bun. 2010. *Lives in the Balance: Improving Accountability for Public Spending in Developing Nations.* Washington, DC: Brookings Institution Press. http://www.brookings.edu/press/Books/2010/livesinthebalance.aspx.

Keefer, Philip, and Stuti Khemani. 2011. "Mass Media and Public Services: The Effects of Radio Access on Public Education in Benin." Working Paper 5559, World Bank, Washington, DC. http://www-wds.worldbank.org/servlet/WDSContentServer/WDSP/IB/2011/02/07/000158349_20110207095259/Rendered/PDF/WPS5559.pdf.

Khan, Asmeen, and Sara Giannozzi. 2011. "Strengthening the Governance Dimension of Social Safety Nets in ASEAN." Unpublished manuscript, World Bank, Washington, DC. http://siteresources.worldbank.org/SOCIALPROTECTION/Resources/SP-Discussion-papers/Safety-Nets-DP/1116.pdf.

Khemani, Stuti. 2007. "Can Information Campaigns Overcome Political Obstacles to Serving the Poor?" In *The Politics of Service Delivery in Democracies: Better Access for the Poor*, ed. Shantayanan Devarajan and Ingrid Widlund. Stockholm: Ministry of Foreign Affairs. http://siteresources.worldbank.org/DEC/Resources/Khemani_CanInformationCampaignsOvercome.pdf.

Koziol, Margaret, and Courtney Tolmie. 2010. *Using Public Expenditure Tracking Surveys to Monitor Projects and Small-Scale Programs: A Guidebook.* Washington, DC: World Bank. http://elibrary.worldbank.org/content/book/9780821385197.

Leventhal, Howard, Robert Singer, and Susan Jones. 1965. "Effects of Fear and Specificity of Recommendation upon Attitudes and Behavior." *Journal of Personality and Social Psychology* 34 (July): 20–29. http://www.sciencedirect.com/science/article/pii/S0022351407607353.

Odugbemi, Sina, and Taeku Lee. 2011. *Accountability through Public Opinion: From Inertia to Public Action.* Washington, DC: World Bank. http://siteresources.worldbank.org/EXTGOVACC/Resources/Accountabilitybookweb.pdf.

Pande, Rohini. 2011. "Can Informed Voters Enforce Better Governance? Experiments in Low-Income Democracies." *Annual Review of Economics* 3: 215–37. http://www.annualreviews.org/doi/abs/10.1146/annurev-economics-061109-080154.

Pandey, Priyanka, Ashwini R. Sehgal, Michelle Riboud, David Levine, and Madhav Goyal. 2007. "Informing Resource Poor Populations and the Delivery of Entitled Health and Social Services in Rural India." *JAMA* 298 (16): 1867–75. http://jama.ama-assn.org/content/298/16/1867.full.pdf.

Rogers, F. Halsey, and Margaret Koziol. 2011. "Provider Absence Surveys: A Guidance Note." World Bank, Washington, DC.

Serra, Danila, Abigail Barr, and Truman Packard. 2011. "Education Outcomes, School Governance, and Parents' Demand for Accountability: Evidence from Albania." Policy Research Working Paper 5643, World Bank, Washington, DC. http://imagebank.worldbank.org/servlet/WDSContentServer/IW3P/IB/2011/04/27/000158349_20110427084959/Rendered/PDF/WPS5643.pdf.

van Stolk, Christian, and Emil Tesliuc. 2010. "Toolkit on Tackling Error, Fraud and Corruption in Social Protection Programs." Social Protection Discussion Series 1002, World Bank, Washington, DC. http://siteresources.worldbank.org/SOCIALPROTECTION/Resources/SP-Discussion-papers/Safety-Nets-DP/1002.pdf.

World Bank. 2003. *World Development Report 2004: Making Services Work for Poor People*. New York: Oxford University Press; Washington, DC: World Bank. http://imagebank.worldbank.org/servlet/WDSContentServer/IW3P/IB/2003/10/07/000090341_20031007150121/Rendered/PDF/268950PAPER0WDR02004.pdf

CHAPTER 2

Social Accountability in the World Bank's Human Development Portfolio

World Bank–financed projects in the human development (HD) sectors support a diverse set of social accountability interventions to inform and motivate citizens to influence service delivery. A portfolio review found that most HD projects approved in FY2005–FY2010 make reference to accountability.[1] Fewer, however, directly finance social accountability measures or incorporate them into their project design, and those that do often face delays in implementation. Although social accountability instruments are not new, they are specialized approaches that involve a learning curve for clients and World Bank staff.

The portfolio review conducted for this study included taking stock of how projects supported by the World Bank incorporate efforts to inform citizens about service delivery and mechanisms for redress. It provides a snapshot of what is happening in the World Bank HD portfolio, including patterns across the HD sectors and the various regions. The exercise included both a review of project documents, mainly project appraisal documents (PADs), and surveys of staff. It therefore misses nonlending activities, which also provide technical and analytical support to governments for social accountability interventions.

Some caveats about the PAD review are important to state upfront. The review looked at project design and thus misses detail on some of the social accountability mechanisms that may be specified in other project documents, such as operational manuals. It also does not include information about project implementation and what actually happened in practice.[2] It is also important to note that World Bank loans support national programs, so the social accountability measures are often not project specific, but rather are part of the government program. Finally, the review did not look in depth at how social accountability instruments have influenced overall project quality.

Most World Bank–supported projects in HD make some reference to accountability and citizen involvement in their documentation. A search of the 427 World Bank projects mapped to the HD sectors that were approved between FY2005 and FY2010 found 380 projects that included at least one of the key words related to accountability (figure 2.1). Of the 380 projects, 20 had 50 or more accountability references—5 of these in health, 2 in education, and 13 in social protection. Looking across regions at the projects including six or more key words, one finds that the regions with the most projects referencing accountability were Africa (84 projects), Latin America and the Caribbean (55), and South Asia (34). Fewer references were found in Europe and Central Asia (27), East Asia and the Pacific (22), and the Middle East and North Africa (8).

The review found no strong trends over time in the number of HD projects that incorporate social accountability measures, but did find a

Figure 2.1   Distribution of Social Accountability Key Words by HD Sector

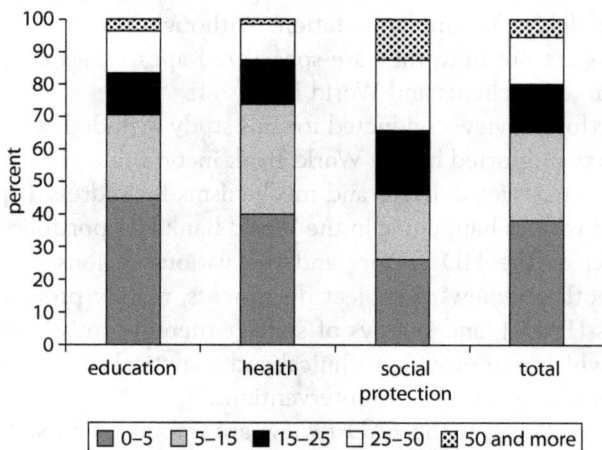

Source: Independent Evaluation Group (IEG) Project database; authors' calculations.

slight increase in the number of references found in the education and health sectors. Half of the health sector projects that were approved in 2005 included at least one accountability-related key word, and this number rose to 65 percent in 2010. Over time, social protection consistently has had the highest incidence of accountability-related key words.

The main conclusion from the stocktaking, however, is that although a large number of HD projects make reference to accountability, fewer incorporate concrete measures into project design. Only 38 financed social accountability in some way. Of these 38 projects, 9 were in education, 12 in health, and 21 in social protection. A subset of these are cross-sectoral: examples include the Kenya Youth Empowerment Project, the Nigeria Community Development Project, and the Dominican Republic Performance and Accountability of Social Sectors development policy loan (DPL). In terms of distribution across regions, Africa has the largest number of projects incorporating social accountability components in the design (16 projects), followed by Latin America (9) and South Asia (8).

The review found that social accountability measures are most common in social protection projects. This result stems from the focus on participation and community-driven development incorporated into many social fund projects that require community members to propose projects and apply for grants from the fund. Social fund projects commonly include information campaigns to stimulate demand for local subprojects and forms of community-based monitoring, such as social audits, to ensure that subprojects are implemented as planned. Social protection projects supporting social assistance commonly include information campaigns to inform potential beneficiaries about their rights and eligibility processes and grievance redress mechanisms for reporting inclusion and exclusion errors.

In the 38 projects identified in the portfolio review (referred to here as the "shortlist"), information campaigns are the most common element found in the shortlist of projects, followed by grievance redress (figure 2.2). Information campaigns are included in a diverse set of projects and take different forms. For example, the Ethiopia Protection of Basic Services (PBS) project publicizes local budget information to citizens, including an extensive budget literacy training program discussed further in chapter 3. Similarly, in Kenya's Secondary Education Project, schools are required to display information on budgets, enrollments, exam results, and number of staff. The Romania Social Inclusion project uses information campaigns to try to encourage higher take-up of social benefits by members of Roma households, who are frequently

Figure 2.2   Social Accountability Measures in HD
percentage of projects included in the "short list"

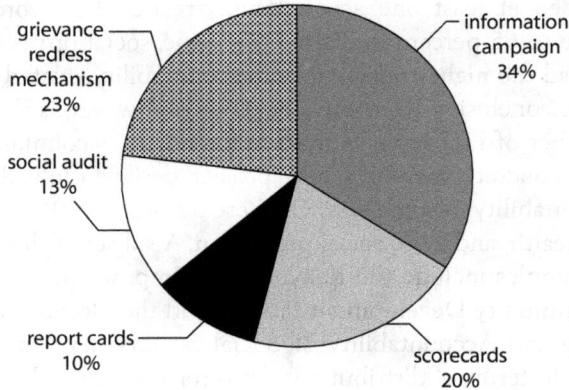

Source: IEG Project database.

excluded from services and may otherwise not know about the program. The Dominican Republic Social Protection Investment Project proposes an ambitious information campaign to increase access to social services for broad categories of stakeholders, including the undocumented population and marginal groups. The campaign aims to be accessible to local communities by providing information in grocery stores and churches and through the radio and mobile speakers.

Grievance redress mechanisms are most common in social protection projects—both social fund projects, such as the Rwanda Third Community and Living Standards Credit DPL, and cash transfer programs, such as the Bolivia Children and Youth Project, which supports a new conditional cash transfer program. The project notes the need to improve the program's transparency, enhance its credibility, and register and respond to complaints as part of its monitoring and feedback processes. The Panama Red de Oportunidades Project includes similar mechanisms for the conditional cash transfer program that it supports, including provisions for feedback channels such as hotlines, web pages, program liaisons, and beneficiary committees. Local committees, which link beneficiaries and social service providers, are also intended to work as feedback channels between beneficiaries and the program's administration.

Some projects also incorporate grievance redress mechanisms to increase the internal accountability of implementing agencies and to mitigate the risks of error, fraud, and corruption in financial management and procurement. The Third Social Action Fund Project in Malawi provides for an anticorruption bureau to oversee the project delivery systems of implementing agencies and to undertake investigations on complaints or allegations of fraud and corruption where needed. Grievance redress mechanisms also appear in education and health projects, mainly those that target funds to individuals, communities, or facilities. The Pakistan Sindh Education Sector Project includes a system for collecting and managing complaints for three subprograms: teacher recruitment, secondary school stipends to female students, and free textbook distribution to public school students. The Kenya Total War against AIDS project has a national hotline for fielding complaints.

Recent HD projects also make use of more active information interventions such as community scorecards and social audits. At least 11 projects in the HD portfolio use scorecards, mostly as pilot efforts (table 2.1). For example, the Ethiopia PBS project includes community scorecards, report cards, and a mechanism for handling complaints. The Malawi Social Action Fund (MASAF) began experimenting with scorecards in 2005, which tracked satisfaction with project management processes; project outputs (such as numbers of water points, classroom blocks, and so forth); the performance of local authorities and MASAF management; and perceptions on the sustainability of MASAF-funded projects.

Lending operations are only one channel for the World Bank to support social accountability. In addition are analytical and advisory activities (AAA),

Table 2.1   Scorecards in Current HD Projects

Project (approval date)	Sector
Angola Local Development Project (2010)	Social protection
Dominican Republic Performance and Accountability of Social Sector DPL I (2009)	Social protection
Ethiopia Protection of Basic Services II Project (2009)	Human development
Madagascar Sustainable Health Systems Project (2007)	Health
Malawi Social Action Fund II Project (2008)	Social protection
Maldives Integrated Development Project (2005)	Health
Nepal Health Sector Program (2004)	Health
Nepal Second HNP and HIV/AIDS Project (2010)	Health
Second Northern Uganda Social Action Fund Project (2009)	Social protection
Senegal Education for All Project (2007)	Education
Tanzania Second Social Action Fund Project (2005)	Social protection

Source: Authors, based on the shortlist of HD projects that went to the Board in FY2005–FY2010.

policy dialogue, and coordination with other donors and civil society. The RECURSO (Rendición de Cuentas para la Reforma Social) program in Peru is an example of a multiyear program of analysis and policy dialogue in the HD sectors that has supported information campaigns to inform citizens about their rights and performance standards (see chapter 3).

Implementation Issues in the Shortlist

Implementation of social accountability measures can be difficult. Staff members working on the shortlist of projects reported delays in implementation in a number of cases.[3] According to the staff survey, social accountability components in one-third of the shortlisted projects were delayed, one-quarter were under implementation, and 11 percent were completed (figure 2.3). Survey respondents identified a number of common bottlenecks both on the side of clients and on the side of the World Bank.

On the client side, a main challenge is that social accountability measures involve concepts and approaches that take time to understand—particularly at the local level. For example, in the Pakistan Sindh education project, it was noted that the introduction of grievance redress involved a change in mindset for government officials, as it implied a shift from a top-down management approach to a more open approach that encouraged the participation of beneficiaries.

Figure 2.3   Implementation Status of Social Accountability Components
percentage of the shortlist

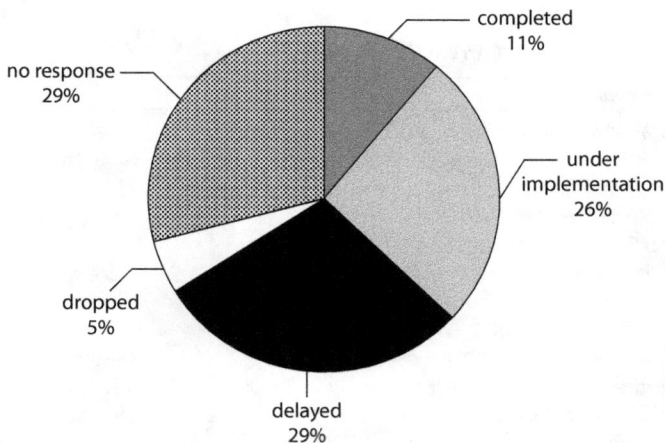

- completed 11%
- no response 29%
- under implementation 26%
- dropped 5%
- delayed 29%

Source: Survey of task teams.

Adopting new ideas and approaches can require additional efforts. The project team in the Dominican Republic hired a civil society expert to improve the quality of implementation of a scorecard initiative at the local level. In Nigeria, the Community and Social Development Project had to build capacity of local organizations on communication and project planning.

World Bank staff members singled out procurement delays and the challenge of donor coordination as reasons for lags in implementation. It is not clear whether these two concerns pose unique problems in implementing social accountability measures or whether the delays are general symptoms of project implementation. Staff members working on projects in Kenya and Pakistan reported that implementation of social accountability mechanisms was delayed because of cumbersome procurement processes, which made it difficult to hire firms quickly for initial activities such as baseline data collection.

Institutional Arrangements

Another key operational question concerns who is in charge of implementation. In some cases, information campaigns are the explicit responsibility of governments, while others that aim to support third-party monitoring—such as scorecards—are deliberately implemented outside of government, through civil society organizations. Because they serve as formal channels between citizens and providers, grievance redress mechanisms are generally built into government or sometimes into project structures. Social accountability measures in World Bank–supported projects include a range of different types of institutional arrangements.

Within the shortlist of projects, staff members reported 18 cases where a government ministry or agency is implementing the social accountability component and 6 cases where civil society organizations are leading implementation. Most projects involve a combination of roles for government and civil society. For example, in the Nepal Second HNP (health, nutrition, and population) and HIV/AIDS project, a government ministry is implementing a social audit, and civil society organizations are piloting and facilitating a community scorecard. In the Kenya Youth Empowerment Project, a nongovernmental organization (NGO) is implementing social audits under the supervision of the Ministry of Youth Affairs and Sports. In Senegal, the government is creating a new communication directorate that will take the lead on implementation.

The staff survey suggested three broad types of institutional arrangements. First, a government ministry along with donor partners and civil society organizations set up a project management unit or committee to implement social accountability interventions; second, the ministry delegates the implementing responsibilities to the district or local governmental units to manage the day-to-day implementation; and third, the implementation of specific tools is directly delegated to civil society organizations that manage ongoing processes. There is no clear guidance to date on what works for the various types of interventions. The effectiveness of these institutional arrangements is an important area for further work.

Among the questions raised by the discussion of institutional arrangements of social accountability interventions in World Bank–supported projects are the extent to which they are "owned" by governments, whether they will be sustained over time, and whether they will influence accountability of service delivery once the project ends. Unfortunately, the limited body of experience and the difficulties of measuring and attributing impact make it hard to draw conclusions.

Most of the information interventions and grievance redress mechanisms included in projects are pilots, and few have been scaled up as yet. An exception is the health scorecard initiative in Madagascar (see chapter 3), which was piloted under a World Bank project and which the government is planning to scale up. World Bank projects also support scaling-up of grievance redress and some information interventions in cash transfer programs. In Colombia and the Philippines, World Bank–supported projects finance the strengthening and expansion of grievance redress mechanisms and social accountability measures of conditional cash transfer programs.

Summary

Projects in the HD sectors have the potential to serve as a laboratory of experimentation with social accountability interventions. Evaluating and documenting these experiences can help to improve the use of these tools in the future. Learning from these experiments means that more and better evaluations are needed (discussed in appendix 1), as well as the building of performance monitoring indicators into projects.

The good news is that the evidence base is set to grow. There are forthcoming evaluations of information interventions within the context of World Bank projects that are testing, among other issues, the effectiveness of different types of information campaigns in Indonesia, the handling of complaints for a conditional cash transfer program in Panama, and score-cards in health and education in the Arab Republic of Egypt and Nepal. The portfolio review also points to the importance of focusing on how social accountability mechanisms contribute to the overall logic of the project's objectives, as well as the feasibility of implementation, including sustainability. These issues are discussed further in the concluding chapter.

Notes

1. The methodology used for the review of the portfolio is described in appendix 2. The review refers to projects supported by the World Bank and the shortlist World Bank projects. It is important to note that these projects are designed, implemented, and owned by the borrowing clients, with World Bank support.

2. This review was not able to look in detail at the quality of the projects and the contribution of social accountability components to overall project quality. A review of the overall project quality ratings in the Implementation Status Reports (ISRs) found that 17 of the projects were rated "satisfactory"; 14 "moderately satisfactory; 2 "moderately unsatisfactory"; and 1 "unsatisfactory." ISRs were not available for five projects in the shortlist. Two were dropped, and three did not have documentation in the project portal. Data were not available for reviewing the quality of the individual components that incorporated social accountability measures.

3. The survey did not ask whether other components of the projects also were delayed.

CHAPTER 3

Informing Citizens

Citizens need information to make smart choices about health care, where to send their children to school, and whether to apply for social benefit programs. They also need information to assess whether policy makers and providers are doing their jobs, delivering quality services, and making effective use of public funds. Instruments for increasing accountability through greater transparency and access to information (ATI) include making information a right through the passage of ATI legislation and micro-level interventions. These mechanisms may include information campaigns to tell citizens about their rights and the standards of service delivery they should expect and scorecards that engage communities and providers around information about the performance of services.

Access-to-Information Legislation

A growing number of countries are adopting legislation—in their constitutions or in separate national laws—providing for access to information about public services and transparency. Although the jury is still out about whether having an ATI framework makes a difference in the quality of public services, such legislation can provide a formal channel for citizens and civil society organizations (CSOs) to request information. ATI legislation provides a legal framework for citizens to become informed about their rights, service standards, and performance of service delivery. It can also be the legal basis for the more active information interventions that are discussed further in this chapter.

ATI can be specified in law in four broad ways.[1] First, it can be part of a country's constitution and usually establishes a *right* to information. Access to information is currently specified in the constitutions of at least 49, and arguably 56, countries.[2] Of these, at least 43, and arguably 50, expressly either specify a right to information (generally) or specific documents or impose an obligation on the state to make information available to the public. Second, 80 countries have a specific ATI law that provides more detail on the extent of the access. India's Right to Information Act (RTIA) is an example. Third, many countries, in particular those with federal systems, such as Canada, Mexico, and the United Kingdom, may have specific regional or local ATI legislation. Fourth are the laws specific to different sectors, such as the environment, which may specify ATI in those areas as a matter of public good or in the national interest. These four approaches are not mutually exclusive, and different countries may have different combinations. Canada, for example, has all four types of legislation.

A review of national ATI legislation carried out as background for this book did not find any country with specific sectoral ATI legislation relating to health or education (DGRU 2011).[3] This finding is in contrast to the environment, where some countries do have separate laws on information access. Most countries consider health and education under the broader umbrella of public information to which citizens would have access under their constitutions or other national ATI laws. This difference raises the question of whether and how having a framework ATI law matters for service delivery (box 3.1).

For enforcement, countries can be classified into three kinds of ATI regimes, which are based on what options people have to request information (Neuman 2009). These regimes are (1) redress through judicial review, (2) redress through an information commission or appeals tribunal with the power to make binding orders, or (3) redress through an information commissioner or ombudsman with the power to make recommendations. Experts do not agree on the most effective combination of ATI regime and enforcement.

Box 3.1

Measuring Access to Information in Education and Health

The World Bank and Global Integrity, a nongovernmental organization, have developed a set of indicators for assessing transparency and access to information at the sector level in health and education.[a] The indicators were tested in the former Yugoslav Republic of Macedonia and collected in Kenya and Ukraine in 2011. The survey uses an expert assessment methodology based on interviews with health and education providers and users of services. The indicators are clustered around four dimensions of information access to relevant health and education service delivery:

- ***Basic issues around the existence and usability of information.*** Assesses the availability, accessibility, and usability of information on health and education services, including whether information on quality of performance is user friendly and accessible and whether information is standardized in a way that makes it comparable across providers.
- ***Redress mechanisms.*** Looks at the availability and accessibility of mechanisms and institutions for handling complaints and estimates of the time taken to lodge a complaint.
- ***Availability of fiscal and budgetary information.*** Looks at the availability of basic fiscal and budgetary information that would theoretically allow local citizens, often through CSOs and media, to monitor service delivery resource flows and the allocation of funds.
- ***Citizen participation in local decision making.*** Examines the existence and effectiveness of formal consultative mechanisms and other informal mechanisms that could theoretically convey citizens' concerns to policy makers in an effective way.

The indicators map what information exists about rights, institutions, and mechanisms and whether health- and education-related information is provided to the beneficiaries of services. The data for FYR Macedonia show a considerable gap between information access laws as they relate to education and health service delivery and their implementation and enforcement. Although a substantial portion of the relevant legal framework is in place, significant work remains to be done to ensure that legislation is effectively implemented.

(continued next page)

Box 3.1 *(continued)*

Further, in FYR Macedonia, the public has the legal right to access school budgets, but this right is regulated by a budget law rather than a law on education. Consequently, although budgets are made available to the public, they do not provide full details such as an itemized list of budget allocations. The data found a similar disconnect with regard to complaint mechanisms: an ombudsman law exists and provides a redress channel, but it is not widely used for health and education services. Instead, people are more likely to complain informally to family and their local networks.

Note: a. Details are available at http://commons.globalintegrity.org/2011/01/new-data-information-access-in-health.html.

Does Having ATI Matter?

A question relevant for this book is whether—and how—having ATI legislation may matter for service delivery in the human development (HD) sectors. The short answer is that there are no clear answers or evidence to date. A recent set of case studies of ATI implementation in five countries looks at three factors (Dokeniya forthcoming). First, promotion of the law is important because substantial investments and changes in the behavior of public service providers are necessary to facilitate information provision and to create awareness among citizens to use the law. Second, oversight and monitoring are needed to ensure implementation of the law. And, third, implementation requires the existence of appeals mechanisms with authority to impose sanctions to investigate denial of requested information. A 14-country study (not specific to the HD sectors) undertaken by the Open Society Institute in 2006, however, found that in some cases, countries that did not have ATI laws had a higher incidence of response to information requests than those that did. The study also found no significant difference between those with ATI laws and those without for access to government information. This finding suggests that laws themselves may be inadequate and that the gaps between legislation and implementation are substantial.

A study in India found sizable gaps on both the demand and supply sides of information provision. Citizens in rural areas, and those with lower incomes and from vulnerable groups, were less likely to use the RTIA. That finding is not surprising because awareness of the RTIA was higher in urban than in rural areas—45 percent of randomly selected respondents in urban areas (state and national capitals) knew about the RTIA (RaaG 2009). In only 20 percent of the more than 400 focus group discussions conducted in villages was there even a single person who knew about the RTIA. The study also found that the RTIA is used predominantly by wealthier and better-educated citizens.

The study found the lack of resources and capacity to be a constraint to implementation. Three-quarters of state-level information commissions reported that they were financially dependent on funds from the state governments, and 60 percent did not have the adequate staffing or infrastructure to carry out their duties. In addition, 40 percent of public information officers, in both rural and urban areas, reported that they lacked training to deal with information requests. The study also noted that the variation in rules and procedures to file RTIA applications across states creates a complex and confusing situation for citizens. One of our colleagues experienced this problem (box 3.2).

Box 3.2

The RTIA in India: A Personal Experience

One of our team members used the RTIA to request information in a dispute surrounding a family land purchase. This experience provides a snapshot of the complexity and limits of the RTIA process. To obtain information under the RTIA, citizens have to write a letter with their information request and pay a nominal fee to cover costs of photocopying or printing. The amount required varies depending on the rules set by specific state governments. The method of payment also varies by state. In some cases, the applicant has to provide a bank draft or a postal order to pay the request for information fee. Such provisions may discourage people from seeking necessary information, as access to banks may not be easily available to everyone.

The family had initially paid a government-managed cooperative society to purchase land in the southern city of Chennai, India. According to the initial agreement, the society was supposed to allot 2,400 square feet of land for an amount of Rs 100,000 (approximately US$2,000). Soon after receiving the payment, however, the cooperative society reduced the initial offer to 1,200 square feet for the same amount. The family asked why this change was made, but received no response. Further, the cooperative was unwilling to reimburse part of the payment due to inflation. The family decided to formally request information from the cooperative society through the RTIA.

(continued next page)

Box 3.2 *(continued)*

The family consulted a local CSO that assists petitioners in drafting letters and provides information on filing an RTIA request. This information was not readily available in an easy form. To get information, the family had to provide a written letter along with a check for Rs 50 to cover the costs of information provision. Because of unclear rules, the family initially addressed the request letter to the deputy registrar of the cooperative society. It was then instructed to write to the special officer in charge of information provision within the cooperative society. The process had to start over again. Upon receipt of this letter, the special officer requested that the family meet with the officials in the cooperative society and settle the issue amicably instead of providing the necessary documentation to reveal the reasons for their change in land size.

Suspecting malpractice and fraud by the cooperative society, the family followed the advice of the CSO and wrote a separate letter to the state information commissioner's office. Within two weeks after receipt of the letter, the commissioner's office called the parties in for a hearing before a panel of three retired civil servants. The panel recommended that the cooperative society either reimburse half of the money to account for the reduction in the land size offered or provide the original agreed amount of land. Because the panel did not have a legal mandate, its decision was nonbinding. It therefore advised legal action in court if the cooperative society did not abide by its recommendation. The cooperative society agreed to reimburse half the amount paid toward the purchase of land. The family was not clearly told why the originally agreed-on 2,400 square feet was not available. Although the process resolved the matter, it did not clarify the reasons behind the sudden change in the amount of land that was being sold—the subject of the original information request.

Source: Authors.

A recent study, however, found India's RTIA to be an effective mechanism for the poor to access ration cards provided under the country's food subsidy program, the Public Distribution System (PDS) (Peisakhin and Pinto 2010). In an experiment conducted with slum dwellers in New Delhi, people who submitted a request for information soon after applying for ration cards received their benefits almost as fast as those who paid a bribe to get their application processed more quickly. In this study, participants were randomly assigned to two groups. One group of participants paid a bribe to a local official via a middleman to speed up their PDS ration card application process, and another group of participants used the RTIA to submit an information request on their pending applications soon after sending in their applications. Those paying a bribe had the lowest median processing time of 2.5 months; the RTIA applicants received their ration cards in 4 months. The control group waited nearly a year (343 days) to receive their cards.

Thus, when citizens can take advantage of ATI provisions, they can benefit from improved services. But how can ATI procedures be made more accessible? One approach could be to standardize procedures for information requests, as has been done in Mexico. The federal information commission, the Instituto Federal de Acceso a la Información Pública (IFAI), has set up a standardized application procedure that users can access through the commission's website.[4] All applications are made to the information commission, which then processes requests.

In 2009, 105,000 information requests were filed in Mexico under the country's ATI law, and according to data from the federal government, the government agencies responded to approximately 96 percent of the requests.[5] If an information request was denied, the requestor could appeal to the IFAI, the body in charge of overseeing implementation. Between 2003 and 2010, the IFAI received 30,833 appeals and ruled against the requester in 18 percent of the cases. Some of the more prominent rulings included disclosure of expenditures on jewels and dresses for the first lady, deviation of resources allocated to the treatment and prevention of HIV/AIDS to pro-life organizations, and mismanagement and embezzlement of resources of large government trust funds.

Although the documentation of how ATI works for individuals overall is limited, there are examples of civil society and the media using ATI mechanisms to investigate service delivery failures (box 3.3). Countries with strong civil society institutions, such as India, Mexico, and Romania, appear to have more extensive ATI legislation because of the ability of civil society to influence policy makers to draft effective laws and to create awareness among citizens about how to use ATI legislation.

The experience from India and elsewhere suggests that simply having ATI legislation is not sufficient; rather, implementation is what matters. Governments need to make the channels for requesting information accessible, transparent, and easy for all segments of the population to use. The media and civil society can promote the adoption and use of ATI and help people file requests and navigate processes. On the supply side, ATI implies changes in the way government officials and service providers share information and interact with citizens, but introducing new

Box 3.3

Civil Society and the Media: Use of ATI in Health and Education

The following examples demonstrate the variety of success of ATI programs:

Hospital waiting lists in Croatia. Transparency International (TI) reports that Croatians believe the health sector to be among the most corrupt sectors in the country, and instances of patients paying bribes to reduce time spent on waiting lists are thought to be fairly common. To address this problem, the Ministry of Health embarked on a pilot to publish waiting lists. The measure obliged hospital executives to disclose lists to patients showing them their position in the line. With the help of TI Croatia, waiting lists at the pilot sites (two major hospitals in Zagreb) were published in 2004 and 2005. TI Croatia set up a hotline to monitor the effectiveness of the initiative, but it is not clear the extent to which people made use of it. In the first few months, the hotline had received only 90 calls about the Dubrava Hospital waiting list. Nevertheless, a patient who had waited two years for heart surgery was operated on within two weeks after lodging a complaint with TI Croatia.

Access to education in Thailand. This case involved Sumalee Limpa-ovart and her daughter Nattanit. When Nattanit was denied admission to a prestigious school because, as officials informed her, she had failed the entrance exam, Sumalee used new ATI legislation in Thailand to request that the school release the exam results, which they eventually did after two years, without names. The results showed that one-third of those who were admitted to the school had failed the exam. Sumalee "suspected that these students were *dek sen*—children from privileged families who used social connections or 'tea money' to gain access to the publicly funded school" (Roberts 2006). When the Thai Supreme Court eventually ordered the school to disclose the names of these students, the information showed that Sumalee's suspicion was correct. The case, which was widely reported in the media, had far-reaching repercussions, eventually resulting in all public schools in Thailand being ordered to reform their admissions policies to bring them in line with the constitutional guarantee against discrimination on social or economic grounds.

Source: DGRU 2011.

procedures and changes to organizational and provider behavior takes time to work effectively.

As a growing number of countries adopt ATI legislation, more analysis is needed, but the limited information that exists to date suggests the need for social accountability mechanisms to complement and supplement the legal framework, especially at the sectoral level. These mechanisms can involve information campaigns, as well as channels for redress if citizens are denied access to information. These interventions are discussed in the following sections.

Information Campaigns

Governments and CSOs have been using information campaigns to inform citizens about their rights, their entitlements, and the standards of services they should expect. These campaigns aim to increase access and use of services by letting people know about the services and programs available to them and to arm people with information that they can use to hold providers accountable for delivering those services. Citizens can use information to have better-informed direct interactions with individual providers, such as physicians, and with provider organizations, such as village education committees, and they can have better-informed indirect interactions with policy makers, including through voting.

Information campaigns for accountability generally provide citizens with two main types of information: (1) their rights, entitlements, and the content, including financing and budgeting, and organization of benefits and services, and (2) the quality and performance of service providers. The latter can refer to the performance of individuals—for example, doctors, teachers, or students—and institutions such as schools and hospitals. Information campaigns generally focus on the first category, and more active information interventions, such as scorecards and social audits, generate information about perceptions of quality and performance from recipients and sometimes providers.

Information about Rights and Entitlements

A common objective of an information campaign is to educate citizens about what services and benefits are available, what they are eligible for, and how to apply for or access those services and benefits. People may not be aware of the services, such as social assistance programs, that are available in their community or free health services. They may not be informed of recent policy changes that may affect their eligibility. Information campaigns can be used to inform citizens to stimulate demand for services and assist with choices about which services to access and how, when, and where they can access them.

Because the lack of information can be a constraint to take-up, social protection information campaigns are common in areas where poor households need to know how and where to apply for benefits such as social assistance cash transfer programs. Information campaigns for social assistance programs are often implemented by local program officials to inform beneficiaries and potential beneficiaries about their rights under the program; rules and processes, including compliance with the requirements for conditional cash transfers (CCTs); and payment schedules and methods (box 3.4).

Box 3.4

Bolsa Família: Information on Social Services, Programs, and Rights

Brazil's flagship CCT program, Bolsa Família (Family Allowance), covers 12.7 million beneficiary families (about 25 percent of Brazil's population). The program relies on diverse approaches to inform people about their rights and obligations under the program and emphasizes that receiving benefits and good-quality social services is a right. Social workers and professionals from the Municipal Secretariats of Social Assistance and the Social Assistance Centers (Centros de Referencia de Assistencia Social—CRAS) promote and implement the program. These agents work with vulnerable families and conduct home visits in poor neighborhoods to search for families that do not seek assistance.

The Bolsa Família program has been well advertised through the main website of the Ministry of Social Development (MDS), local radio ads, and pamphlets and posters that are distributed around poor neighborhoods and public offices. Just one year after the program was launched in 2004, Bolsa Família enrolled 1.6 million new beneficiary families. This number, combined with the households enrolled in programs that merged into Bolsa Família, meant that the program reached 6.6 million families in its first year.

The MDS continued its information campaigns, and the media promoted debate about the concept and delivery of CCTs. During 2006, an average of one article per day appeared in key newspapers, most of them with positive coverage

(continued next page)

Box 3.4 *(continued)*

(Lindert and Vincensini 2010). By the end of 2006, the program had 11.1 million beneficiary families.

Once a family is admitted in the program, social assistance professionals send notification and provide guidance on how the program works, explaining aspects such as (1) the program's objectives, (2) the concept of conditionalities and the family's responsibilities to receive benefits, (3) the consequences of noncompliance, (4) the payment process, and (5) contact information for additional questions and for reporting any irregularities. The main instrument that summarizes these guidelines is known as the *Agenda da Família*, which is provided to all new beneficiary families. The MDS encourages social workers to follow up proactively with beneficiary families and update their registries every two years or less to record changes in family composition, change of address, and other relevant information. In addition, the MDS mandates special assistance to families that are not complying with the conditionalities to help them avoid disqualification.

The MDS and municipalities advertise their payment calendars and other important information through posters and radio ads. The program also communicates with beneficiaries when they withdraw their benefit at the bank. For example, if a family has not complied with a specific conditionality and withdraws money from the program, it may receive a request on the withdrawal receipt to contact a social worker from CRAS to resolve the situation before benefits are temporarily blocked or canceled.

Bolsa Família has also improved its outreach to highly disadvantaged groups, such as indigenous populations, *quilombolas* (African descendant groups), and the homeless, with targeted efforts that include (1) adapting Bolsa Família materials into local dialects and using appropriate graphic design to address each groups' culture, (2) training local agents on how to reach each group, and (3) reviewing the Cadastro Único's registry form to capture more detailed information on each vulnerable group.

Source: Fruttero, Gomez, and Ringold 2011.

Information about Service Standards

Information campaigns can also let people know about national or local standards for service delivery and enable citizens to demand better services. For example, in education, a growing number of countries participate in international learning assessments that allow for benchmarking across countries. Such information can be used to pressure policy makers and providers for better results (Bruns, Filmer, and Patrinos 2011). If parents know average test scores across schools or those associated with individual teachers, they may use the data to choose where (or whether) to send their children to school. The information could also encourage them to demand changes from their existing schools.

In Peru, a program of information campaigns—known as RECURSO (Rendición de Cuentas para la Reforma Social)—informed parents about rights to education, health, and nutrition and what standards they should expect. The program started with campaigns in education. In spite of high primary enrollments in education, a study found that of 136 randomly selected second grade children, 35 percent were unable to read a single word, but 80 percent of parents surveyed were satisfied with the quality of education their children received. This gap between true learning levels and perceptions of quality suggested a lack of awareness of quality standards and potentially weak accountability in school management.

In 2006, the government of Peru established a universal standard system to test all children completing second grade and to inform each school, child, and parent about the results by issuing report cards through local education offices. Media campaigns encouraged parents to request their child's test scores from schools and discuss the results with the school authorities to plan improvement strategies.

One of the products was a radio miniseries about education standards and parental empowerment, produced in Spanish and translated into the indigenous languages of Quechua, Aymara, and Asháninka. The government also linked teachers' pay to evaluation as part of the education sector reform process. In spite of opposition from teacher unions, the government was able to pass this law with support from the electorate.

Although an impact evaluation is not available, improvements in education that coincided with the RECURSO program have been impressive. Follow-ups to the 2006 assessment of second graders found that the proportion of students classified in Level 0 was down from 46 percent to 30 percent in 2007 and to 23 percent in 2009; at the same time, the percentage of children in Level 2 rose from 16 percent in 2007 to 23 percent in 2009 (Vinadio 2010). In the absence of an impact evaluation, however, it is not possible to assess whether these improvements can be attributed to RECURSO and, if so, to which specific aspect of the initiative.

Following the program on education rights and standards, RECURSO supported similar efforts to inform parents about child nutrition and health services. Parents were told that their children should grow at least

24 centimeters in their first year, and at least 12 centimeters in their second. By setting expectations and by introducing an understanding of the right to services to help them achieve a set outcome, this intervention aimed to equip parents with information so that they could question policy makers and providers about the services their children received.

Information about Budgets and Financing

Information interventions that aim to improve provider accountability frequently give information to citizens about the level and allocation of public funding for services. The goal of this type of information is to help citizens understand how public resources are being used and estimate what they should expect of their local providers. Such information can be made available through the media, including newspapers, radio, or the Internet, or it can be provided directly through accessible bulletin boards at a service facility or local government office.

Public expenditure tracking surveys. These surveys, known as PETS, are tools to track the flow of public resources (including human, financial, or in-kind) from the highest levels of government to frontline service providers (Koziol and Tolmie 2010). They can help civil society and policy makers to understand funding flows, identify areas of leakage, and make informed policy decisions based on their findings (Griffin et al. 2010). PETS employ an extensive mapping exercise to understand the flow of funds through different levels of government. Once the resource flows are mapped, budget data are collected and analyzed and are often complemented with a facilities survey and qualitative research. CSOs, governments, and donors, including the World Bank, use PETS to assess the amount of leakage in funds allocated by federal government to subnational governments or to facilities (box 3.5).

PETS can be valuable tools for accountability, but they are neither simple nor inexpensive to implement; instead, they are demanding exercises that require attention to detail from design through to communicating the results. They can be particularly challenging for CSOs to implement without assistance because they require technical expertise and skills to collect and analyze data and because governments may be unlikely to grant CSOs and researchers access to data, particularly about budgets and financing. Sometimes, however, it is possible for CSOs to do expenditure tracking on a large scale. In India, a nongovernmental organization (NGO), the Accountability Initiative, manages a program that tracks school grants in more than 13,000 government schools. Data are

Box 3.5

Accountability and the Use of Public Expenditure Tracking Surveys

Through analysis and advocacy, the Transparency and Accountability Program (TAP) of the Results for Development Institute provides technical and financial support to civil society organizations involved in promoting accountability in public service delivery in developing countries. Since 2006, TAP has supported at least 22 PETS and absenteeism studies in 18 countries in Africa, South Asia, Eastern Europe, and Latin America. Following are two examples of projects led by TAP-supported civil society organizations:

Responding to a call from a newly elected minister of education to improve education during her first 100 days in office, the Centro de Investigaciones Económicas Nacionales (CIEN) in Guatemala designed a PETS to identify problems in six primary school financing programs, including support for textbooks and school meals. Although CIEN found little leakage during its study, the organization did identify significant delays in the distribution of resources to schools. Interviews and focus group discussions carried out in conjunction with the study allowed researchers to diagnose the possible cause of the delays: a school calendar that overlapped with the fiscal calendar, which led to bottlenecks in approving resource allocation and delivery to schools. CIEN presented these findings to the Ministry of Education, which led to the decision to shift the school calendar in 2009 to address the delays.

The government of Kenya introduced the Secondary Education Bursary Fund in 1993. The fund was intended to ensure that students, particularly those living in poverty, were able to attend and stay in school, thereby reducing disparities in secondary school education. In 2008, the Institute of Policy Analysis and Research (IPAR) undertook a tracking survey to assess the level of demand for the scheme and the efficiency of the scheme in the eight districts encompassing Nairobi. IPAR uncovered significant delays in the funding, poor targeting, and deficiencies in recordkeeping, and the Ministry of Education requested an expanded nationally sampled study, which was completed in 2010.

Source: http://tap.resultsfordevelopment.org.

collected by citizens who are trained by CSOs to be "barefoot expenditure trackers."[6]

Translating the findings into policy action is another challenge. Even the best designed and analyzed expenditure survey may fail to have an impact if it is not effectively communicated to government officials and the public through an information campaign. Creative communication methods can help CSOs increase public interest in budget problems. The Centre for Budget and Policy Studies (CBPS) in India offers an example. The CBPS often uses films about governance and public expenditure management to introduce people to the ways budgeting has a direct impact on their daily lives. Methods and tools such as cartoons, posters, and videos can all be used to increase interest in budgeting. The Accountability Initiative publishes accessible budget briefs on expenditures on public services.[7]

Newspaper campaign in Uganda. A newspaper campaign in the education sector in Uganda presents an example of how a PETS can be used to increase accountability in the allocation of public funds (Reinikka and Svensson 2004, 2011). In 1996, the Ugandan government administered a PETS targeting government primary schools and found that on average only 13 percent of a capitation grant for non-wage expenditures from the central government was reaching those schools.[8] In response, the government implemented an information campaign that published data in national newspapers on the monthly amounts of capitation grants that were supposed to go to all schools. In 1997, they extended this effort by requiring primary schools and district administrations countrywide to post notices on actual funds received in a public space where all people would have access to the information.

A follow-up PETS was conducted in 2002 and showed a remarkable improvement in head teachers' knowledge of the grant program, which in turn increased the percentage of funds that reached the schools. To test the impact of the newspaper campaign, the authors compared schools with greater exposure to newspapers (proxied by distance to the nearest newspaper outlet) to schools with less exposure to newspapers and therefore less exposure to the information campaign. They showed that head teachers in schools farther away from newspaper outlets knew less about the timing and release of funds. They then used distance from the newspaper to predict the amount of information that head teachers had (that is, distance is used as an instrumental variable for information) and found that a 1.0 standard deviation increase in information led to a 1.1 standard deviation increase in spending that reached the schools (meaning a 44.2 percent increase between 1995 and 2001).

This research suggests that schools where headmasters had greater knowledge of capitation grant allocations, entitlements, and leakage received a higher amount of the grant following the information intervention. The study did not, however, examine the impact of the campaign on parents' awareness or involvement and so did not discover whether the newspaper campaign was effective in increasing demand or if it only improved local schools' ability to demand resources from the central government.

Budget literacy in Ethiopia. The importance of demystifying budget processes and enhancing financial literacy is also incorporated into government programs. The Ethiopia Protection of Basic Services (PBS) project, financed by the World Bank, supports the government's effort to increase accountability for service delivery through greater budget transparency and by raising the population's financial literacy (IPE Global 2010). The project supports the government's goal of expanding access and improving the quality of basic services in education, health, agriculture, water supply and sanitation, and rural roads. The project includes efforts to make information about budgeting and financing available, as well as training on budget literacy and how to interpret the information.

As part of the financial transparency and accountability (FTA) component, the government publishes detailed fiscal information on the Internet, including quarterly updated federal and regional fiscal data, block grant allocations, and monthly transfers from regions to districts (*woredas*), including their share of revenue. The majority of *woredas* (90 percent) post their budgets in public places. In addition to the Internet, a wide range of media are used, including radio and television, as well as distribution of calendars, T-shirts, and other materials. The FTA has even commissioned poems and dramatic pieces to promote the program. At the local level, *woredas* have set up opinion boxes for gathering citizens' comments and complaints. In addition, because literacy is low in Ethiopia, the government has designed simplified visual tools that use minimal text and numbers to convey information on planned and actual budget expenditures at the *woreda* and facility levels.

Complementing the information campaigns, the Ethiopian government is implementing training in budget literacy to help citizens understand basic concepts in the financing and delivery of services and then provide feedback about their priorities. The initiative provides training to regional and local government officials, staff from sector offices and CSOs, journalists, and the public. As of May 2011, more than 47,000 citizens had participated in the training. Participation of women in the budget training was initially low and is being increased through targeted efforts. So far the program's impact has not been evaluated, but reports from some of the participating regions suggest that people are using information to demand services. Students in Amhara requested textbooks after learning that books were available but had not been distributed. And in the same region, citizens also filed complaints about the performance of capital investment projects—including schools and health posts.

Information about the Organization of Service Delivery

Information campaigns can also tell people how they can be more involved in service delivery, including opportunities to participate in parent-teacher associations, and how to file a complaint. In developing and developed countries alike, citizens may be unaware of the existence of these types of participatory governance mechanisms for service delivery. Informing people about these channels can facilitate citizen involvement and grievance redress, especially in decentralized environments. In many countries, public services are partially overseen by individuals who are either elected or appointed by the community. For these arrangements to work, those involved in community oversight need to be informed of their roles and responsibilities. Two experiments in education in India found contrasting results from campaigns to inform people about local governance arrangements.

Information campaign in Uttar Pradesh. In a randomized experiment, an information campaign in the north Indian state of Uttar Pradesh in 2005 assessed the impact of providing information about village education committees (VECs). In the local village schools, the VECs were responsible for managing some operations, such as administering grants from the central government and hiring and firing local contract teachers (Banerjee et al. 2010). One of the main assumptions behind one of the interventions was that people did not know about the VECs, and a baseline survey indeed revealed that many VEC members themselves were unaware of their roles or responsibilities.[9] Some were not even aware that they were members! Parents often did not know about the presence of such a committee.

The study worked with a prominent NGO, Pratham, to administer the information intervention. Pratham activists spent several days facilitating group discussions in each of the village neighborhoods and inviting those neighborhood groups to a larger villagewide discussion with teachers and village administrators. The administrators shared information about the structure and organization of public service delivery, especially the role of VECs. The meetings were followed by distribution of leaflets that described the various responsibilities of VECs.

Overall, the information intervention did little to change parent awareness or involvement, teacher effort, or student absenteeism, and three to six months later, learning outcomes had not improved. Members of the VEC, however, had become slightly more aware of their roles and responsibilities.

Although there could be numerous explanations for the limited results, two conditions prevailed prior to the interventions that might have suggested that parents would not respond to a mobilization effort to improve school performance or learning in public schools. First, students themselves were absent from school more than 50 percent of the time, so education may not have been a high priority for parents in these areas. Second, 37 percent of interviewed parents had already checked out of the public school system altogether and enrolled their children in private schools. This information suggests that it should not be surprising that service users were unaware of the governance arrangements in their educational establishments.

Information campaign in Uttar Pradesh, Madhya Pradesh, and Karnataka. The second study—also a randomized intervention—was conducted in 2006–07 in three states in India: Uttar Pradesh (UP), Madhya Pradesh (MP), and Karnataka (Pandey, Goyal, and Sundararaman 2007). Information about state-mandated roles and responsibilities in school management was disseminated through a series of village meetings, and the campaign made use of tools such as short films, posters, wall paintings, calendars, and learning assessment booklets that contained information on minimum learning standards for language and math.

The study found different levels of impact on outcomes related to teacher effort, entitlement receipt, and student learning in the three states. In UP, teacher attendance increased by 11 percent, but there was no significant change in the amount of time teachers spent on classroom instruction. In MP, teacher attendance did not change significantly, but teachers' instruction time in the classroom increased by 30 percent. In Karnataka, the effects of the information campaign on teacher attendance and classroom instruction time could not be statistically distinguished from zero.[10]

The interventions also led to varied results in awareness and the receipt of entitlements. In UP, girls were more likely to receive school uniforms, and the oversight committees met more often throughout the school year, including parent members. Parents were also more likely to participate in school inspections and talk to a VEC member or teacher about the quality of education. Other entitlements, such as textbooks, school meals, and student stipends, did not increase, aside from the stipend received by students who did not come from marginalized caste or tribal backgrounds. In MP, only girls from marginalized castes and tribes were more likely to receive scholarships, and parents were more likely to talk to a teacher about the quality of education. The study found no improvement in any other outcomes. In fact, relative to the control group, the VECs held fewer meetings throughout the school year. In Karnataka, students reported slightly better-quality school meals, and parents were more likely to meet with the school oversight committee, but no other entitlements or parental involvement outcomes increased significantly.

Learning impacts were scattered and fairly small. Grade 3 students in UP, for example, were three percentage points more likely to read sentences and words, and grade 4 students in Karnataka were more likely to recognize words. Other skills, such as writing sentences and doing addition, subtraction, division, and multiplication, did not improve, and all other sets of students (grades 2 through 4 in MP, grades 2 and 4 in UP, and grade 5 in Karnataka) made no progress. This information campaign implemented in three different parts of India led to some positive impacts, but it is clear that the impact was not consistent across states either in magnitude or in which kind of service delivery was affected: teacher effort, student learning, or parent awareness and involvement.

Information about the Quality and Performance of Services
The idea behind many social accountability approaches is that equipping users with information about quality and performance of services can help them pressure providers for better results. If parents know average test scores across schools or those associated with individual teachers, they may be able to choose where (or whether) to send their children to school. The information could also encourage them to demand changes from their existing schools. In the United States, hospitals use report cards to communicate comparative information about performance (box 3.6).

Report cards in Uttar Pradesh. In another randomized intervention in UP that built on the information campaign to inform citizens about the roles and responsibilities of the VECs, facilitators organized discussions around the quality of education (Banerjee et al. 2010). A simple literacy test was conducted to assess students' reading levels, and the test scores were shared with parents, teachers, and VEC members to give everyone

Box 3.6

Report Cards in Health

Report cards are used for reporting performance of health facilities in Organisation for Economic Co-operation and Development countries. A 1989 New York State public report on cardiac surgery publicized wide variations in mortality rates among providers. Following its release, lower-rated hospitals responded by improving cardiac surgery departments, and one of the poorest-performing hospitals achieved distinction in 2002 by having the lowest risk-adjusted mortality rate of any hospital in the state.

A later evaluation of the New York reform found that this report card effort decreased the number of cases seen at lower-performing hospitals and at the same time led to quality improvements at those same facilities.

Sources: Chassin 2002; Cutler, Huckman, and Landrum 2004.

a clear picture of the current state of education quality in the village. Information collected at baseline revealed that parents and VEC members tended to overestimate student abilities. But even when citizens were trained to create report cards on their children's learning levels, this kind of more active engagement did not did not spur them into action, change teacher effort, or improve learning outcomes.

School report cards in Pakistan. A randomized experiment of school report cards in Pakistan seemed to change the relationship between providers and parents. A major feature of this study was that the researchers included all the schools in all the villages involved, which allowed for the intervention to affect the entire education market in a village (approximately seven schools on average per village), and each village was randomized into treatment or control. The purpose of the report card was to provide information to parents and schools regarding the academic performance of children both on an absolute scale and relative to other children and other schools. A teacher's version of the report card included a more detailed breakdown of scores by subject so teachers could identify the areas that needed improvement. The report cards were handed out to parents, accompanied by a discussion about the factors affecting a child's score so as not to assign blame to the children and to help illiterate parents understand the information in the report cards.

This study estimated that the report cards led to positive impacts within the education market. First, average test scores increased by

0.10 standard deviations in both public and private schools. Second, private schools with baseline scores below the median had the largest learning gains—0.34 standard deviations. Third, private schools with above-median initial scores showed no learning gains but dropped their fees by 23 percent. It is important to note that these impacts took place within a reasonably competitive market (seven schools per village, considerable private sector presence), and it is not clear if the results would have been the same had the market consisted of only government schools or a smaller set of schools.

Reporting on performance in North Carolina. In the United States, the No Child Left Behind Act of 2001 stipulated that children attending failing schools be given the choice to attend nonfailing schools outside of their neighborhood. The plan assumed that parents would choose to send their children to better-performing schools when given an opportunity to do so. Some studies in North Carolina suggest, however, that low-income families placed less weight on academics when choosing where to send their children to school, leading to fewer gains when they did switch schools (Hastings, Kane, and Staiger 2006).

A natural experiment and a field experiment in a North Carolina school district examined the degree to which the format of information affected parents' choice of schools. Prior to 2004, the school district allowed parents to submit their top three school choices each year for their child and provided information about schools in a guide that included self-descriptions and positive attributes of each school. The guide ran longer than 100 pages. If parents wanted objective statistics on academic achievement, they could access a website where they would have to make tedious comparisons school by school. In 2004, following the initial school choice process for that year, the school district sent parents a three-page alphabetical printout of test scores of every school in the district.

In an additional field experiment that also included parents from nonfailing schools, a one-page information sheet sorted the schools by their ranking, listed their odds of admission, and limited the set to the schools in parents' neighborhoods.

Both the three-page form and the ranked one-page form led parents to send their children to better-performing schools. When given the test score information about schools in the three-page format, parents who had initially chosen to switch schools changed their choices to schools with test scores an average of 0.50 standard deviations higher than their previous choices, and the proportion of all parents whose children attended failing schools who chose to send their children to schools outside their assigned neighborhood increased by five percentage points.

The results from this natural experiment, however, mix the effects of information about the relative quality of schools and learning that a particular school has been labeled as failing. In the field experiment, some of the households in the treatment and control groups did not have children in failing schools. To get at the pure effect of information, the researchers compared the parents who received the one-page information sheet to their counterparts, who received nothing. The former were 7.5 percentage points more likely to choose a different school when they received the report card on the schools in their area and the chosen school had test scores 0.1 standard deviations higher on average. Thus, information helped them choose a better school for their children. The researchers found no additional advantage of the one-page form over the three-page form.

"Active" Information Campaigns: Scorecards and Social Audits

Instead of simply providing and interpreting information for beneficiaries of services, information interventions such as scorecards and social audits actively involve community members in collecting information about service delivery, reporting on provider performance, discussing concerns with providers, and making decisions. These approaches aim to engage communities to act collectively to influence providers and policy makers. Scorecards and social audits involve face-to-face meetings between citizens and providers. The assumption is that the scrutiny and monitoring by communities will alter the incentives of providers either through reputational repercussions or the simple act of being observed.

Some of the evidence, however, suggests that community participation may improve outcomes only when community members have a comparative advantage in making decisions. In infrastructure projects in northern Pakistan, increasing community participation in nontechnical decisions—for example, wages for community labor during project construction or the distribution of project benefits—improved project maintenance, but increasing participation in technical decisions, such as project scale or time frame for project construction, worsened project outcomes (Ijaz Khwaja 2004).

Some of the interventions previously discussed included elements of active engagement between citizens and providers. Similarly, PETS can be implemented by civil society organizations and involve users of services in data collection. There is a growing body of experiments with these types of instruments in both developing countries and Organisation for Economic Co-operation and Development (OECD) countries. This section discusses examples of scorecards and social audits and identifies lessons for further work in this area.

Scorecards

In a randomized experiment with scorecards in the health sector in Uganda, communities were encouraged to come up with a plan to identify problems and to draft a community action plan for improving service delivery together with providers (Björkman and Svensson 2007). Although the training lasted only a few days, and the responsible external organization made only one follow-up visit after six months, health outcomes improved dramatically after one year, as did more intermediate outcomes, such as provider effort and community-monitoring activities.

Each treatment facility and its community had a unique report that summarized the findings from surveys on the quality of services in their area. These report cards were translated into the local language, and posters were designed to present complicated information in a pictorial form to community members with low levels of literacy. The results were presented through a series of meetings, including a community meeting, a staff meeting, and a face-to-face meeting with providers. On average, more than 150 people attended the community events, where the facilitators used maps, diagrams, role play, and focus group discussions to disseminate the information in an easily understandable manner.

Because one of the main objectives was to also help the communities use the information to enforce accountability and demand better services, the facilitators showed people how to formulate action plans. The action plan summarized the community's suggestions for improvement and areas needing attention. Common issues that arose were high rates of absenteeism, long waiting times, weak attention from the health staff, and differential treatment. The health providers' staff meetings were held at the health facilities, and the providers' information was compared with data on the community's perceptions. The comparisons helped providers review and analyze their performance and compare it with other clinics in the district. Finally, a meeting was organized that brought the health facility staff together with participants chosen by the community from the villages. The face-to-face meeting devised a strategy for improving health service provision based on the action plan produced during the community meeting and discussion during the health facility staff meeting.

The community scorecard project as a whole led to significant improvements in health outcomes and health-seeking behavior: a 33 percent average reduction in infant mortality and a 20 percent increase in utilization. Child immunization rates also increased.

Some of these improvements may have been mediated by changes in provider effort. Health worker absence decreased by an average of 13 percentage points (from a baseline rate of 47 percent), waiting times went down an average of 12 minutes, and providers were 8 percentage points more likely to use equipment during their examination (from a baseline rate of 41 percent). Some of the improvements in health outcomes and provider effort might also have been mediated by increases in community monitoring. Treatment communities were 32 percentage points more likely to have a suggestions box (from a baseline of 0 percent), 16 percentage points more likely to have numbered waiting cards in the clinic (from a baseline of 4 percent), and 27 percentage points more likely to have a poster informing patients which services should be free (from a baseline of 12 percent).

It is unclear, however, to what extent increases in provider accountability can account for all of the improvements in health outcomes and provider effort. The intense focus on health outcomes and entitled services during the scorecard exercise could have stimulated demand for health services, and providers might have improved their services after learning that the services were not as effective as they thought. (Appendix 1 discusses learning about why programs worked.)

Social Audits

Social audits allow citizens receiving a specific service to examine and cross-check the information the service provider makes available against information collected from users of the service. This form of monitoring could cover all aspects of the service delivery process, such as funds allocated, materials procured, and people enrolled. The audit results are typically shared with all interested and concerned stakeholders through public gatherings, which are generally attended by users of the services as well as public officials involved in management of the service delivery unit.

Social audits in the National Rural Employment Guarantee Act in India. Social audits have been institutionalized as a tool for monitoring program effectiveness in the National Rural Employment Guarantee Act

(NREGA) in several states in India (Chamorro et al. 2009).[11] The NREGA program was introduced in 2006 as a flagship social protection program that guarantees 100 days of employment per year to rural households whose adult members are willing to do unskilled manual work. An innovative feature of NREGA is that it assigned social audits as a means of continuous public vigilance. The government of Andhra Pradesh set up a separate unit to design and implement social audits of the NREGA program. The core of the social audit approach is to involve the entire affected group or community in the process. In most cases, the members carrying out the social audits are volunteers who are directly affected by the program, and these volunteers are generally trained in the social audit process by a civil society organization.

The World Bank and the government of Andhra Pradesh surveyed 840 NREGA households in three districts of the state three times in seven months (Pokharel et al. 2007). In addition, another 180 participants were interviewed five to seven days after the social audit. Between the first and third visit the survey found a large increase in the percentage of the NREGA participants who knew about the program and its details. The percentage of people who knew that the program provided 100 days of work went up from 31 percent during the first round to 99 percent in the third round. The number of participants reporting entries in their job cards also went up after the social audits, suggesting participants had understood the importance of documentation. Because these estimates are simple before and after comparisons, they cannot be considered the causal impact of the social audit, but their magnitude suggests that the social audit did improve awareness among potential participants.

Community scorecards in Madagascar. Although community scorecards are increasingly popular across the World Bank's HD portfolio, most are pilots. The example of scorecards in Madagascar is unique because they are in the process of being scaled up with help from the Ministry of Health as part of the health monitoring system of SanteNet, one of the largest health NGOs in Madagascar (Brinkerhoff and Keener 2003; World Bank 2007, 2010).

The scorecards were initially piloted to monitor and improve the quality of health services. Madagascar suffers from high rates of absence among health providers, as well as challenges related to centralized human resources management, which leaves district health offices with limited authority to address performance issues. The 2007 Poverty and Social Impact Analysis on health found that in the rural areas, which make up more than 70 percent of Madagascar, users were turning to the private sector as an alternative to public health services.

Between late 2006 and 2008, community scorecards were piloted in two phases in 26 primary health centers in four regions: Analamanga and Haute Matsiatra in the central highlands and Boeny and Anosy on the coast. After a pause in activity during a political crisis, the scorecard process is currently entering its third phase—a scale-up of scorecards through SanteNet.[12] Phase 1 of the scorecard intervention tested the applicability of the methodology and adapted the tool to the Malagasy context. Phase 2 tested methodological and implementation strategies to increase the cost-efficiency of scaling up, improve results monitoring by incorporating tracking of objective indicators, and increase effectiveness of the tool.[13]

The Malagasy scorecard process involves six steps:

1. Preparation, during which all community members are publicly informed via radio and as many local contacts as possible about a public meeting, and during which objective baseline data are collected on each health post
2. Random sampling (numbers picked from a hat) of participants from the public meeting for user evaluations of different aspects of service and simultaneous provider evaluations of service quality
3. A face-to-face meeting three to five days later between health care providers and the population where the evaluation results are compared and the norms and limitations of service are discussed and shared with community members
4. Development of a local action plan to address any deficiencies and designation of an existing or new team to follow up on the action plan
5. Publication at the regional level of results from the various scorecard exercises, including press coverage and feeding of the information back to the Ministry of Health management and to regional authorities
6. Repetition of the cycle three to four months later to evaluate changes.

The Design and Implementation of Information Campaigns

The success of information interventions rests not only on what information is conveyed, but also on how it is conveyed. This book emphasizes that it matters how information interventions are designed and implemented. For information campaigns, success depends on considering what information is presented and how. Accessibility of information campaigns is also a key to success. Concentrated efforts may be needed to ensure that the poor and excluded groups are reached. The RTI Assessment and Analysis Group study on access to information in India showed that people living in rural areas and the poor are less likely to file ATI requests, and the reason may be that they do not know about them (RaaG 2009).

Delivery and Implementation

Some of the information campaigns discussed previously make significant efforts to deliver information in accessible formats. For example, in the Ugandan health scorecard intervention, the information cards used during the scorecard process were translated into local languages and included pictures that would be more accessible to illiterate community members. Facilitators also used methods such as maps, diagrams, role play, and focus group discussions. And in Ethiopia, the budget literacy campaign included in the PBS program emphasized making financing information accessible to the public.

Information campaigns use a diversity of formats and are becoming more technologically savvy with the increased use of mobile phones and the Internet. The examples already discussed employed tools ranging from the mass media, including the newspaper campaign in Uganda, to personalized report cards about student and school test scores in Pakistan. The three-state study of education campaigns in India used a short film, poster, wall painting, calendar, and a learning assessment booklet for communication. What methods work best remains to be determined.

Evaluating information campaigns in Indonesia. An ongoing evaluation in Indonesia is testing whether national, district, or more local campaigns are the most effective form of communication for an education-related information campaign.[14] The campaigns aim to increase communities' awareness of recent reforms—namely, the introduction of school committees and, in 2005, the national School Operational Grant (BOS) program, which provides block grants to public and private schools on a per student basis. Every school in Indonesia should have a school committee, with a membership of at least nine people drawn from parents, community leaders, education professionals, the private sector, teachers, community-based organizations, and village officials.

The BOS grants on average amount to more than 50 percent of a school's operational budget and are intended to finance school operations and reduce the burden of fees charged to parents. Each school committee is expected to monitor the use of BOS funds and assess whether it furthers the school's development plan. A 2009 survey found that although a large share (86 percent) of parents had heard about the BOS program, fewer knew its objectives (45 percent), very few had ever participated in school planning (less than 10 percent), and only 7 percent had ever looked at a BOS expense report.

In response, the government, with the support of the World Bank, has been piloting different approaches to increase awareness of BOS and parental involvement in the allocation of BOS funds. The campaign has three tiers, with increasing levels of direct interaction with parents and communities.

The first tier is countrywide, with public advertisements in national television stations and newspapers.

The second tier is at the district level and emphasizes how proper BOS management requires transparency, accountability, and stronger collaboration between school and parents. These campaigns include a districtwide social event to disseminate BOS information and promote teacher-parent collaboration, media relations and advocacy, and local radio and TV programs.

The third tier of the campaign zeros in on the school. It places BOS notice boards in schools, texts parents regularly with information on BOS, sends regular letters from schools to parents to provide information on BOS, and conducts school meetings. Local school committees participate in this tier of the campaign. These different campaign approaches were rolled out experimentally, and their relative effectiveness will be evaluated.

School report cards in Cambodia. A well-intentioned experiment with report cards in the context of a World Bank–financed education project in Cambodia underscores what can happen if an information campaign is not implemented successfully. The Cambodia Education Sector Support Project (CESSP) included school report cards with the objective of raising school accountability. The report cards aimed to present the community and students with information on school performance that would allow them to benchmark their expectations for the school and demand better services.

Ultimately, the Ministry of Education Youth and Sport discontinued the experiment. Although the information required for the report card was clear and comprehensive, much of it was not easily collected at school level in Cambodia. As a result, some of the report cards were incomplete, which undermined the community members' abilities to compare their schools' results with others in the district or province. In addition, the cards were primarily text and numbers, with no graphics or pictures, and did not accommodate the parents who could not read.

The Presentation of Information

The design of campaigns, including how information is presented, can influence success. Evidence from disciplines ranging from psychology to marketing—and most recently behavioral economics—underscores that framing the message makes a big difference for the effectiveness of information campaigns. In one interesting example, research from Brazil found that *telenovelas* (TV soap operas) that portray strong, independent women who have divorced their husbands increased rates of divorce (Chong and La Ferrara 2009). As noted, the education study from North Carolina also showed that parents—especially those from low socioeconomic backgrounds—chose better schools for their children when they were presented with a simple 3-page information sheet about the performance of schools in their neighborhoods that replaced a booklet that ran more than 100 pages (Hastings and Weinstein 2008).

A number of field experiments further demonstrate the importance of message framing. Yale University students noticeably increased their expressed intention to get a tetanus shot when presented with information booklets that conveyed the consequences of contracting tetanus and the benefits of inoculation in a way that was intended to elicit fear—with graphic pictures of hospital patients and tetanus sufferers and dramatic language—compared to students who had seen the same information presented in a less dramatic way (Leventhal, Singer, and Jones 1965). Voters are similarly susceptible to framing. In Benin, when a politician's platform on education, health, and development was described as part of a national program, the candidate received fewer votes than in villages where the campaign stressed the politician's ethnic identity and the platform was portrayed as a method for transferring resources to the region (Wantchekon 2003).

Experiments with financial institutions show how the framing and presentation of messages can elicit sizable changes in saving behavior and decrease financial vulnerability in low-income settings. When a large payday lender in the United States expressed its lending fees and those of alternative forms of credit, such as credit cards, car loans, and subprime mortgages, in a way that facilitated direct comparisons, clients reduced the amount they borrowed from the payday lender (Bertrand and Morse 2010).[15] Borrowing against future paychecks decreased even further when the lending fees of the lender and alternative credit sources were expressed in dollar amounts rather than interest rates and when the total accumulated fees for a hypothetical loan outstanding for two weeks to three months were tabulated. In a set of experiments in Bolivia, Peru, and the Philippines among clients with savings accounts, text message reminders that stressed the clients' saving goals—for example, with a picture of what they were saving for or with a jigsaw puzzle piece after each deposit—increased saving more than simple reminders (Karlan et al. 2010).

Summary

This review of information interventions points to a number of considerations for further use of such interventions in the HD sectors. First, the legal and institutional setting for access to information, including the existence of ATI legislation, can establish a framework for citizens and civil society to access information about public services. On its own, however, ATI legislation is unlikely to influence accountability of service delivery. Passing a right-to-information law does not guarantee that information will be made available to citizens unless there are specific campaigns to let people know about their rights, about the standards and performance they should expect, and how to file a request. These themes are discussed further in the next chapter on grievance redress.

Second, access, especially for poor and excluded groups, is an essential consideration for all types of information interventions. The poor may need assistance in filing information requests and accessing information in general. They may also need assistance and support in understanding information. Civil society organizations, including the media, can be helpful in this area. Third, the importance of design and implementation of campaigns calls for attention to how information is presented and for assurance that campaigns are accessible to poor and excluded groups.

Notes

1. The term *access to information* is used instead of other commonly used terms, including *freedom of information* and *right to information*, as ATI conveys a wider set of considerations, legal and nonlegal, and does not limit consideration of access to information as a right only.

2. See http://right2info.org. The discrepancy in numbers is due to differing definitions of the right to information.

3. Social protection was not included in this review.

4. See https://www.infomex.org.mx/gobiernofederal/home.action.

5. This discussion draws from Dokeniya (forthcoming).

6. Information on the Planning, Allocations and Expenditures, Institutions: Studies in Accountability (PAISA) program can be found at http://www.accountabilityindia.in/paisa-planning-allocations-and-expenditures-institutions-studies-accountability.

7. See http://www.accountabilityindia.in/budget-briefs.

8. The same study found that the absence rate among teachers in the sample facilities was 27 percent.

9. The study presented results of three interventions, only one of which is discussed in this section. The other two parts of the study incorporated (1) training of community members in the administration of a simple reading test and the invitation of community members to create report cards on the status of enrollment and learning in their village and (2) training for one or more volunteers in the village on how to teach basic reading skills and delivery of reading classes outside regular school hours to interested students.

10. The study did not present standard errors of the estimated impacts so it is not possible to determine whether the statistically insignificant results should be interpreted as impacts of zero or very imprecise impacts that might be quite large. See appendix 1 for more discussion on the situation of low statistical power.

11. The social audit process has been used in Andhra Pradesh, Orissa, and Rajasthan states in India to monitor effective implementation of the NREGA programs.

12. A U.S. Agency for International Development–supported NGO, SanteNet, which has provided technical support to much of the health care centers, is in the process of integrating a scorecard approach into its work at the commune level (Commune Mendrika program). The initiative was expected to exist in 56 communes by June 2011, and once deemed successful will be scaled up to more than 744 communes.

13. The second phase explored the effectiveness of community-based versus region-based facilitators by dividing facilitators into two types: 10 regional facilitators, possessing strong numeric, analytical, and organizational capacity, and 40 communal facilitators with strong facilitation skills. Each was assessed for effectiveness. Although the community-level facilitators was more effective in organizing follow-up, they were less skilled at the quantitative reporting required to compare results. As a result, the model proposed for scaling up will continue to include regional-level facilitators.

14. This section is based on a case study of BOS-KITA prepared by Rivandra Royono and Sunniya Durrani-Jamal (2011).

15. "Payday lending" refers to small, short-term loans intended to cover a borrower's expenses until his or her next payday.

References

Banerjee, Abhijit V., Rukmini Banerji, Esther Duflo, Rachel Glennerster, and Stuti Khemani. 2010. "Pitfalls in Participatory Programs: Evidence from a Randomized Evaluation in Education in India." *American Economic Journal: Economic Policy* 2 (1): 1–30. http://pubs.aeaweb.org/doi/pdfplus/10.1257/pol.2.1.1.

Bertrand, Marianne, and Adair Morse. 2010. "Information Disclosure, Cognitive Biases and Payday Borrowing." Chicago Booth Research Paper 10-01, Booth School of Business, University of Chicago. http://papers.ssrn.com/sol3/papers .cfm?abstract_id=1532213.

Björkman, Martina, and Jakob Svensson. 2009. "Power to the People: Evidence from a Randomized Field Experiment of a Community-Based Monitoring Project." *Quarterly Journal of Economics* 124 (2): 735–69. http://qje.oxford journals.org/content/124/2/735.full.pdf+html.

Brinkerhoff, Derick, and Sarah C. Keener. 2003. "District-Level Service Delivery in Rural Madagascar: Accountability in Health and Education." Abt Associates, Washington, DC.

Bruns, Barbara, Deon Filmer, and Harry Anthony Patrinos. 2011. *Making Schools Work: New Evidence on Accountability Reforms.* Washington, DC: World Bank. http://siteresources.worldbank.org/EDUCATION/Resources/278200-1298568319076/makingschoolswork.pdf.

Chamorro, Mariandrea, Jasmine Cho, Diane Coffey, Dane Erickson, María Elena García Mora, Payal Hathi, Jenny Lah, and Piali Mukhopadhyay. 2009. "Holding Government to Account: The Case of the National Rural Employment Guarantee Act (NREGA) in Andhra Pradesh, India." Unpublished manuscript, Woodrow Wilson School of Public and International Affairs, Princeton University. http://www.princeton.edu/rpds/announcements/HammerPolicy ResearchReport2010.pdf.

Chassin, Mark R. 2002. "Achieving and Sustaining Improved Quality: Lessons from New York State and Cardiac Surgery." *Health Affairs* 21 (4): 40–51. http://content.healthaffairs.org/content/21/4/40.full.pdf+html.

Chong, Alberto, and Eliana La Ferrara. 2009. "Television and Divorce: Evidence from Brazilian Novelas." Working Paper 651, Inter-American Development Bank, Washington, DC. http://idbdocs.iadb.org/wsdocs/getdocument.aspx? docnum=1856109.

Cutler, David, Robert S. Huckman, and Mary Beth Landrum. 2004. "The Role of Information in Medical Markets: An Analysis of Publicly Reported Outcomes in Cardiac Surgery." *American Economic Review* 94 (2): 342–46. http://pubs .aeaweb.org/doi/pdfplus/10.1257/0002828041301993.

DGRU (Democratic Governance and Rights Unit). 2011. "The Role of National Legislation in Supporting Access to Information in Health and Education." Draft report, University of Cape Town.

Dokeniya, Anupama. Forthcoming. "Implementing Right to Information Reforms: Emerging Conclusions from Case Studies." World Bank, Washington, DC.

Fruttero, Anna, Catalina Gomez, and Dena Ringold. 2011. "Governance in Bolsa Família: Roles, Responsibilities, Coordination, and Accountability." Unpublished manuscript, World Bank, Washington, DC.

Griffin, Charles, David de Ferranti, Courtney Tolmie, Justin Jacinto, Graeme Ramshaw, and Chinyere Bun. 2010. *Lives in the Balance: Improving Accountability for Public Spending in Developing Nations.* Washington, DC: Brookings Institution Press. http://www.brookings.edu/press/Books/2010/livesinthebalance.aspx.

Hastings, Justine S., Thomas J., Kane, and Douglas O. Staiger. 2006. "Parental Preferences and School Competition: Evidence from a Public School Choice Program." Working Paper 11805, National Bureau of Economic Research, Cambridge, MA. http://www.nber.org/papers/w11805.pdf?new_window=1.

Hastings, Justine S., and Jeffrey M. Weinstein. 2008. "Information, School Choice and Academic Achievement: Evidence from Two Experiments." *Quarterly Journal of Economics, MIT Press* 123 (4): 1373–414. http://qje.oxfordjournals.org/content/123/4/1373.full.pdf+html.

Ijaz Khwaja, Asim. 2004. "Is Increasing Community Participation Always a Good Thing?" *Journal of the European Economic Association* 2 (2–3): 427–36. http://www.jstor.org/pss/40004916.

IPE Global. 2010. "Evaluation and Design of Social Accountability Component of the Protection of Basic Services Project, Ethiopia." http://www.ansa-africa.net/uploads/documents/publications/ESAP-Evaluation_Report_June2010.pdf.

Karlan, Dean, Margaret McConnell, Sendhil Mullainathan, and Jonathan Zinman. 2010. "Getting to the Top of Mind: How Reminders Increase Saving." Working Paper 16205, National Bureau of Economic Research, Cambridge, MA. http://www.nber.org/papers/w16205.pdf?new_window=1.

Koziol, Margaret, and Courtney Tolmie. 2010. *Using Public Expenditure Tracking Surveys to Monitor Projects and Small-Scale Programs: A Guidebook.* Washington, DC: World Bank. http://elibrary.worldbank.org/content/book/9780821385197.

Leventhal, Howard, Robert Singer, and Susan Jones. 1965. "Effects of Fear and Specificity of Recommendation upon Attitudes and Behavior." *Journal of Personality and Social Psychology* 34 (July): 20–29. http://www.sciencedirect.com/science/article/pii/S0022351407607353.

Lindert, Kathy, and Vanina Vincensini. 2010. "Social Policy, Perceptions and the Press: An Analysis of the Media's Treatment of Conditional Cash Transfers in Brazil." Social Protection Discussion Paper 1008, World Bank, Washington, DC. http://siteresources.worldbank.org/SOCIALPROTECTION/Resources/SP-Discussion-papers/Safety-Nets-DP/1008.pdf.

Neuman, Laura. 2009. "Enforcement Models: Content and Context." Access to Information Working Paper Series, World Bank Institute, World Bank, Washington, DC. http://siteresources.worldbank.org/PSGLP/Resources/LNEuman.pdf.

Pandey, Priyanaka, Sangeeta Goyal, and Venkatesh Sundararaman. 2007. "Community Participation in Public Schools: The Impact of Information Campaigns in Three Indian States." Unpublished manuscript, World Bank, Washington, DC. http://www-wds.worldbank.org/external/default/WDS ContentServer/IW3P/IB/2008/11/11/000158349_20081111142153/Rendered/PDF/WPS4776.pdf.

Peisakhin, Leonid, and Paul Pinto. 2010. "Is Transparency an Effective Anti-corruption Strategy? Evidence from a Field Experiment in India." *Regulation and Governance* 4 (3): 261–80. http://onlinelibrary.wiley.com/doi/10.1111/j .1748-5991.2010.01081.x/full.

Pokharel, Atul, Salimah Samji, Yamini Aiyar, and Shree Ravindranath. 2007. "Standing Under the Arch: Understanding Social Audits in the Context of the Andhra Pradesh Rural Employment Guarantee Scheme." World Bank, SPIU (Government of Andhra Pradesh), and Intellecap. http://www.rd.ap.gov.in/SAudit/Standing_Under_the_Arch-_V3.pdf.

RaaG (RTI Assessment and Analysis Group). 2009. *Safeguarding the Right to Information: Report of the People's RTI Assessment 2008.* New Delhi: RTI Assessment and Analysis Group and National Campaign for People's Rights to Information. http://www.rtigateway.org.in/Documents/References/English/Reports/8.%20RaaG%20study_exe_summary%20-%20revised.pdf.

Reinikka, Ritva, and Jakob Svensson. 2004. "Local Capture: Evidence from a Central Government Transfer Program in Uganda." *Quarterly Journal of Economics* 119 (2): 679–705. http://qje.oxfordjournals.org/content/119/2/679 .full.pdf+html.

———. 2011. "The Power of Information in Public Services: Evidence from Education in Uganda." *Journal of Public Economics* 95 (7–8): 956–66.

Roberts, Alasdair. 2006. *Blacked Out: Government Secrecy in the Information Age.* Cambridge, U.K.: Cambridge University Press. http://assets.cambridge.org/97805218/58700/frontmatter/9780521858700_frontmatter.pdf.

Royono, Rivandra, and Sunniya Durrani-Jamal. 2011. "BOS-KITA Case Study." Unpublished manuscript, World Bank, Jakarta.

Vinadio, Tommaso. 2010. "Governance and Anti-corruption Case Studies." Unpublished manuscript, World Bank, Washington, DC. http://gacknowl edge.worldbank.org/pro/Resources/GAC%20Results%20-%20Peru%20 Recurso.pdf.

Wantchekon, Leonard. 2003. "Clientelism and Voting Behavior: Evidence from a Field Experiment in Benin." *World Politics* 55 (3): 399–422. http://muse.jhu.edu/login?uri=/journals/world_politics/v055/55.3wantchekon.html.

World Bank. 2007. "Republic of Madagascar Poverty and Social Impact Analysis: Health Care and the Poor." World Bank, Washington, DC.

———. 2010. *Health, Nutrition, and Population Outcomes in Madagascar 2000–2009: A Country Status Report.* Washington, DC: World Bank.

CHAPTER 4

Channels for Using Information: Grievance Redress

For accountability to work, citizens, once they are informed, need opportunities to transform information into action.[1] Grievance redress mechanisms are one channel that citizens can use for accountability, along with others such as choice and voting. Grievance redress mechanisms (GRMs), also known as complaints-handling systems, are the formal institutions and channels people can use to express their dissatisfaction with service delivery and to demand redress. They can also be used in a positive way to give feedback to providers and policy makers about the performance of services. In other words, grievance redress mechanisms are channels for citizens to make use of information to hold providers, program managers, and policy makers accountable for service delivery.

Grievance redress mechanisms generally are conduits for individuals to complain, but they can also reflect collective views if complaints are aggregated and used to inform policy. In most cases, they are also the accountability channels of last resort and used for complaints and grievances that cannot be resolved at the point of delivery.

What Are Grievance Redress Mechanisms?

There are three broad categories of grievance redress mechanisms. The first category is **grievance redress mechanisms within government agencies.**

Within this category are hotlines, complaints offices, websites, and other channels that governments set up to field complaints about their programs and services. These mechanisms can exist at various levels—ranging from the ministry down to the point of delivery, such as within hospitals or social welfare offices. For example, in the United Kingdom, the Department for Work and Pensions has separate complaints departments for each of its subagencies: Pension Service, Jobcentre Plus, Child Support Agency, Debt Management Organization, and Disability and Careers Service.[2]

Grievance redress mechanisms can also be set up within donor projects that support government programs. The design of Kenya's Hunger Safety Net Programme (HSNP) includes GRMs at the community level. At the district level, the HSNP is designed to have a grievance front office to receive complaints. Complaints that cannot be addressed by the district office are forwarded to the national grievances coordinator.[3]

The second category consists of **independent redress institutions**. It includes a diverse set of institutions that operate outside of the formal government bureaucracy, such as tribunals, ombudsmen, civil society organizations (CSOs), and a variety of sector-specific entities, such as labor relations boards. Because they are independent of the government, these types of institutions generally have little or no public authority to enforce their findings, and their judgments are often advisory only.

The third category is the judicial system, primarily the **courts**. Depending on local legal traditions, institutional configurations, and political circumstances, courts can hear complaints and requests for redress regarding the failures of line agencies and providers to comply with their statutory and contractual obligations. Courts can also review the regulations that govern service delivery. In a number of countries— Brazil and Colombia, for example—courts have become notably active in the health sector and are active in shaping access to care.

In practice, grievance redress institutions and processes can be overlapping at the country level. A country may have an ombudsman for citizens to raise general issues regarding the health sector and facility-level channels for registering complaints. The French health insurance system has an ombudsman system through an official and independent conciliateur, who can be contacted through the local health insurance office. The ombudsman's decisions are nonbinding, but are generally respected.[4] The main independent ombudsman, the médiateur de la République, helps settle disputes with civil service departments with a much broader jurisdiction than health or social welfare.[5]

In Mexico, in addition to the court system, citizens have at least three channels through which they can register complaints about Oportunidades, the national conditional cash transfer (CCT) program. The complaints system is operated through the central and local offices of the program administration. Citizens can also register complaints through two federal government offices: the Dirección General de Atención Ciudadana de la Secretaría de la Función Pública (Department of Citizens Affairs in the Ministry of Civil Service), which handles citizens' petitions and complaints for all public services, and the Fiscalía Especializada para la Atención de Delitos Electorales (Special Prosecutor for Electoral Fraud), which reviews formal complaints in all issues related to electoral politics (Gruenberg and Pereyra Iraola 2008).

Nongovernmental organizations (NGOs), the media, and other actors within civil society can be important to enable and facilitate access to grievance redress. This role is similar to that played by CSOs that help people file access-to-information (ATI) requests (discussed in chapter 3). In particular, some NGOs provide legal aid to help the poor and other vulnerable populations petition the court system and other channels for accessing justice. Examples in India include the Human Rights Law Network, Lawyers Collective, and People's Union for Civil Liberties; examples in South Africa include the Legal Resources Centre and the AIDS Law Project (Gauri and Brinks 2008). The extent to which a "culture" or context of grievance redress exists in a country reflects both the extent to which formal channels exist and are used, and the activity of these external actors.

Despite the potential importance of GRMs, the literature on this subject is limited, particularly in developing countries. Reviews of grievance redress in both developing and OECD (Organisation for Economic Co-operation and Development) countries that were carried out for this book found few detailed case studies and no evaluations or empirical studies that looked at the relationship between complaints-handling systems and the quality of service delivery—in human development (HD) and other sectors. Across the HD sectors, grievance redress mechanisms are more frequently found in social protection and health services, where they are commonly integrated into cash transfer programs. They exist to a lesser extent in education.

This chapter first looks at what is known about whether people use GRMs and to what ends. It then looks at what constitutes grievance redress in each of the three HD subsectors. The chapter concludes with

a discussion of design issues, including some of the institutional preconditions for grievance redress.

Do People Use Grievance Redress?

When grievance redress mechanisms are available, do citizens use them?
Given the diversity of mechanisms for grievance redress and the lack of
data, the answer is not straightforward. The extent to which people make
use of GRMs depends on the country context and the types of redress
systems that exist. Countries with more developed legal systems may rely
more heavily on courts for redress, and countries with an active civil society
may make greater use of independent third-party channels for redress.

Studies from Europe find that a relatively small share of the population actually uses complaints-handling systems—either within government agencies and programs or independent redress institutions—and
those who do are often not the vulnerable or disadvantaged (Moyer 1984;
NAO 2008a; Fountain 2001). A recent European Bank for Reconstruction
and Development (EBRD)–World Bank survey of 35 countries in Europe
and Central Asia found that, on average, only 7 percent of respondents
had ever filed a complaint about health and education services (EBRD
2011). Western Europeans were more likely to file complaints than citizens of the transition countries of Eastern Europe and Central Asia (fig-
ures 4.1 and 4.2). These rates were higher in Germany and Sweden,
where close to 30 percent of people mentioned that they had complained
about education, and close to 15 percent about health care.

Fewer than half of the respondents in the transition countries reported
knowing where to file a complaint, but most people in these countries
who did file a complaint reported that they received a response (although
to a lesser extent in Central Asia and Southeastern Europe). About two-
thirds (and more in the Russian Federation) were satisfied with the
response they received.

Examples from the United Kingdom show that even if people say that
they intend to register a complaint, they may not actually do it. The U.K.
National Audit Office (NAO) ran a census in 2005 of service users. Most
users said they would likely make a complaint to remedy a fault or mis-
take in their treatment by a government agency (NAO 2005). Other
studies suggest that the likelihood that people complain is much lower in
practice. The NAO estimated that 14 percent of patients reported being
dissatisfied with health services, but only 5 percent had filed a complaint
(NAO 2008a, 2008b).

Figure 4.1   Have You Filed a Complaint in Education? Responses from Europe and Central Asia

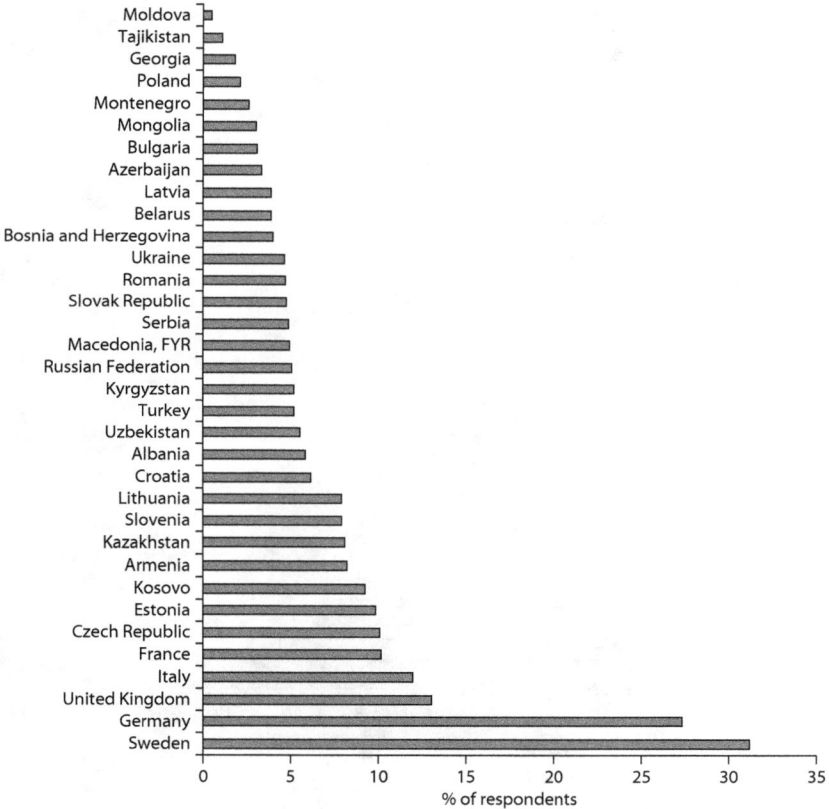

Source: European Bank for Reconstruction and Development and World Bank 2010.

U.K. studies show that the main reason people cite for not complaining is lack of awareness (box 4.1). Other reasons include fear of reprisal (including losing eligibility for benefits), the perception that nothing will change as a result of the complaint, the lack of help in navigating the complaints process, limited awareness of the complaints-handling process, limited understanding due to the complexity of the system, limited understanding due to technical language used, the time and expense required to file a complaint, and the lack of protection for the complainant (GAO 2010; NAO 2005, 2008a).

Reasons for not complaining can vary between specific population groups. An NAO study in 2005 found that young people had particularly

Figure 4.2   Have You Filed a Complaint in Health? Responses from Europe and Central Asia

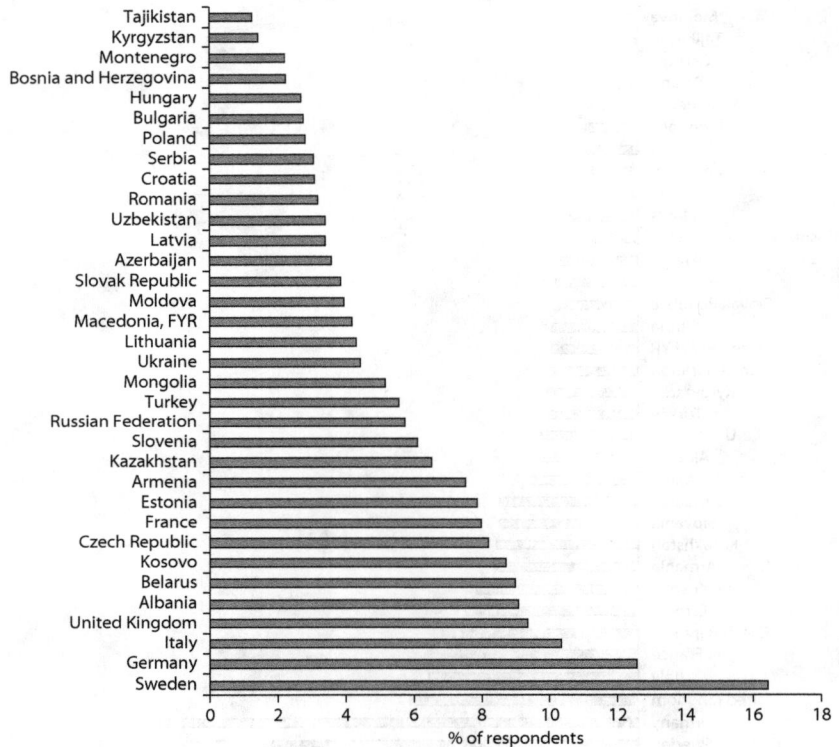

Source: Life in Transition Survey (LiTS) 2010.

poor awareness of how to complain. A study of redress systems in Mexico's Oportunidades program and Argentina's Plan Jefes y Jefas de Hogar Desocupados (Program for Unemployed Male and Female Heads of Households) found that poor households and women were less likely than others to access complaints systems. Although women receive the transfers at a high rate, some have argued that the GRMs are not accessible to women (Gruenberg and Pereyra Iraola 2008).

Once someone files a grievance, what constitutes redress? The answer depends on the context and the type of grievance that has been lodged. The grievance may be a simple one: a man may simply claim a benefit that program administrators have denied him. Others may be more complex. A beneficiary who was improperly denied a social grant might demand interest on top of the grant amount. For corporal punishment,

Box 4.1

Issues with Complaints-Handling in the U.K. National Health Service

A 2008 report by the U.K. National Audit Office of complaints handling in the National Health Service (NHS) identified a number of constraints to access and effectiveness. The main findings cited in the report are as follows:

- *Ignorance about the NHS complaints process,* with a perception that it is lengthy and bureaucratic. The nature of people's experiences with the NHS had to be either very good or very bad to prompt formal praise or criticism, and the greatest barrier to formal complaints was patients' lack of a benchmark by which to judge their experience.
- *Confusion about how to make a complaint,* especially when people are dealing with more than one NHS body at the same time, and difficulty in securing a satisfactory outcome when complaints concern failures of communication or service delivery.
- *Difficulty in navigating the complaints systems* due to the wide range of bodies to which a complainant might reasonably address concerns, and public confusion regarding the dividing lines between primary and secondary care, and health and social care.
- *People feeling intimidated by the NHS* and thinking that their complaint would not be taken seriously. Patients felt uncomfortable about complaining directly to their individual provider and were concerned that it could have serious consequences for their ongoing relationship. Complaints relating to general practitioners are a challenging area as there are limited channels for investigation without cooperation from individual doctors.
- *Lack of a systematic way to learn lessons from complaints,* both about service provision and about complaints handling, and underexploitation of information from complaints as a learning resource and means to identify failures in service delivery.
- *Lack of systems for monitoring and learning from complaints.* Board reports on complaints concentrate on discussing numbers and statistics rather than the content or seriousness of complaints. Although complaints data may lead to one-off changes to service delivery, they are not necessarily shared across trusts or health economies.

Source: NAO 2008a.
Note: References for the individual findings are available in the source document.

a student and his parents might want an apology. A victim of medical malpractice might ask for compensation, along with a reprimand or other punishment of the clinician. An NGO might seek, in addition to redress for harmed members of the community on whose behalf it speaks, a change in policy so that future beneficiaries in the community will not be improperly denied benefits.

The EBRD–World Bank survey showed that most people who filed a complaint about education and health services reported that they received a response. In Western Europe the rate of response was 72 percent for complaints about health and 83 percent for education. Response rates in the transition countries were lower, particularly in Central Asia, where rates were around 45 percent.

Even when redress systems exist, they may not provide resolution. An analysis of grievance redress systems of the cash transfer programs Jefes y Jefas and Oportunidades found that very few of the most serious criminal complaints lodged against the programs actually resulted in sanctions. Oportunidades clients submitted 28,214 claims between 2005 and 2006, and only 7 percent received sanctions. Jefes y Jefas clients submitted 12,151 claims, and 3 percent were sanctioned. Although there is no way of knowing what percentage of cases should have resulted in sanctions without understanding the facts of each case, the study concludes that these low rates suggest that the redress mechanisms are still underdeveloped and lack the capacity to confront clientelism within the programs (Gruenberg and Pereyra Iraola 2008).

In addition to resolving individual complaints and grievances about service delivery, GRMs can provide valuable feedback and information to providers and policy makers for improvements. A promising example from an OECD country is from Denmark's health sector, which aims to aggregate data from its complaints-handling system to improve service delivery. The Danish Institute for Quality and Accreditation in Healthcare works to see that complaints and other incidents are systematically captured, analyzed, and acted upon, and it follows up to evaluate the effectiveness of actions taken. In addition, the Patient Complaints Board is charged with disseminating the board's important decisions, known as decisions of principle. Every year the board distributes its data on around 250 such cases. The website gives access to a database of more than 2,000 decisions of principle. These efforts have been shown to improve the accessibility of complaints-handling systems and increase client confidence in the complaints-handling process (Lister et al. 2008).

An international review of grievance redress mechanisms by the U.K. National Audit Office in nine OECD countries, however, found that learning and synthesizing information from complaints received was not very well integrated across complaints-handling systems (Lister et al. 2008). The review found that health agencies in charge of managing complaints did not make efforts to conduct reviews on the nature of complaints received and make necessary changes to service provision.

Grievance Mechanisms in the Human Development Sectors

Grievance redress mechanisms take diverse forms across the HD sectors. The literature reviews and the survey of World Bank projects undertaken for this book found that GRMs are more common in social protection projects than in health and education. In social protection, GRMs are a common feature in cash transfer programs. In the health sector, courts are growing in importance, and in education, few examples of GRMs were found.

In the context of World Bank–supported projects, grievance redress across the HD sectors largely focuses on the allocation of targeted funds to individuals, communities, and facilities, as mechanisms for facilitating targeting and limiting leakage. This section discusses the forms that GRMs take within the three HD sectors.

Social Protection

Grievance redress is an important element of managing a targeted program, particularly when cash is involved. GRMs can be important for mitigating inclusion and exclusion errors in targeting and for monitoring corruption. Transfer programs usually have complaints-handling systems in place for potential beneficiaries to protest if they thought they were eligible but were denied a benefit; if they received a benefit but believe the amount is wrong; or if they think that someone else—say, a neighbor—is receiving benefits but should not be eligible.

Most of the conditional cash transfer (CCT) programs in Latin America, such as Bolsa Família in Brazil, Familias en Acción in Colombia, and Oportunidades in Mexico, have extensive grievance redress systems that combine redress mechanisms within government agencies, at the national and program levels, with independent redress institutions. Most complaints fielded through CCT programs have to do with benefit payments. In Colombia, 80 percent of complaints about Familias en Acción were related to nonpayment of benefits (Rodriguez Restrepo 2011).

GRMs are found in social protection programs that disburse targeted grants, such as social funds and other community-driven development programs, to poor communities. Grievance redress can also be important for the delivery of social services. In the United Kingdom, a complaints procedure for adult social care has been in place since 1991. Complaints most commonly relate to poor standards of treatment or people not being treated properly, uncaring attitudes of staff members, or inaccurate or misdiagnoses (NAO 2008a).

Grievance redress in Bolsa Família. In Brazil, the complaints system for Bolsa Família illustrates how grievance and information interventions may intersect. The system has four channels: (1) toll-free hotlines managed by the Ministry of Social Development (MDS) that provide information and collect complaints; (2) e-mails and letters sent to the Bolsa Família address, which the MDS processes; (3) complaints made to publicly constituted councils at the municipal level that monitor the program; and (4) a public oversight network. The program in the state of Piaui covers about 400,000 beneficiaries, and in the early phases of the program, its hotline received as many 300,000 calls per month with complaints and requests for information.

The Bolsa Família Secretariat examines complaints and adopts actions according to the level of complexity of each situation. In most cases, the MDS recommends that municipal-level program coordinators review complaints received at the local level. Complaints are also monitored by local social control bodies made up of civil society representatives and local government officials who provide oversight of the program. They have the mandate to follow up on processes and make sure that actions are taken and sanctions adopted, although no information was available about whether this happens in practice.

Philippines CCT program. In the Philippines, grievance redress is an important feature of the Pantawid Pamilyang Pilipino Program (known as the 4Ps), a conditional cash transfer program. The program supports approximately 1 million beneficiary households, and the government planned to scale up the program to 2.3 million households in 2011. Complaints are entered into a publicly accessible database that tracks the nature, origin, location, and status of complaints, including targeting errors, payment irregularities, fraud, and corruption. The database takes in complaints from text messages, various websites, Facebook, Twitter, and a hotline. In the first quarter of 2010, approximately 13,500 complaints were received, and more than 80 percent were related to payments. A survey of one region found that 13 percent of the population had complaints about the program (World Bank 2010). The number of complaints is not surprising given the rapid expansion of the program, which now covers approximately 20 percent of the poor. The complaints system is also an important source of information for course corrections as the program expands.

Program-specific grievance redress mechanisms for CCTs are increasingly being built into the management information systems of the programs. These systems can facilitate tracking and monitoring of complaints received and the ability to aggregate types of complaints to improve the functioning of the program (Silva Villalobos, Blanco, and Bassett 2010). Advances in technology such as text-message-based systems can make the cash transfer programs function more efficiently.

Health

Grievance redress mechanisms in the health sector need to cover diverse issues, such as complaints of malpractice, financing, and access to care. Ministries of health and individual facilities can set up administrative complaints-handling systems at various levels, starting with the clinic. In addition, courts are becoming more involved in grievance redress in a number of developing countries, particularly in Latin America and South Asia.

The World Bank's portfolio does not have many examples of GRMs in the health sector, but two projects in Kenya integrate complaints mechanisms. The Total War against AIDS project has a grievance mechanism, including a national hotline to check the appropriateness of grant-targeting of aid money to CSOs for the prevention and treatment of HIV/AIDS. The Kenya Health Sector Support project incorporates a complaints system that aims to increase provider accountability. The system includes a toll-free hotline, complaints boxes at health facilities, and the opportunity to send complaints to district officials. Complaints are expected to address the following: (1) staff members are not available during the clinic hours; (2) staff members are available, but fail to attend to clients in time; (3) staff members demand additional money beyond the user fees; and (4) all other issues.

U.K. National Health Service. An example of grievance redress that is accessible to patients at the hospital level comes from the U.K. National

Health Service (NHS). The complaints procedure starts with the patient's hospital or primary care trust.[6] A patient has two available services. The first is the Patient Advice and Liaison Service, which is found in each hospital and offers confidential advice, support, and information on health-related matters to patients, their families, and their caregivers.[7] The second is the Independent Complaints and Advocacy Service (ICAS), which provides support to service users who choose to make a formal complaint about the NHS. If a complainant is unhappy with the first decision on his or her issue, the next step is to request a review by the Health Care Commission. If that proves unsatisfactory, the patient can appeal to the health service ombudsman, the ultimate reviewer of NHS complaints.

In 2006–07, the NHS received 133,400 complaints, 32 percent of which were related to primary care services. The NHS employed 880 full-time staff members to handle the complaints. The large majority (94 percent) of complaints were resolved locally. The Health Care Commission accepted 7,696 complaints for independent review. The health service ombudsman reviewed 862 complaints that were not resolved by the NHS or the commission. Despite the existence of ICAS to help people file complaints, a survey conducted in 2007 found that 84 percent of dissatisfied NHS users were unaware that help was available for accessing the complaints service. Reviews of the effectiveness of the NHS complaints system in 2005–06 identified issues of low awareness regarding use of the system and concerns about the timeliness and quality of the responses (see box 4.1).

The role of courts. Since the 1990s, domestic courts, including national supreme courts, have heard larger numbers of cases relating to the right to health, particularly in low- and middle-income countries. The focus of these cases has ranged from access to health services and medication, to protection of the right to health of vulnerable and marginalized groups. An analysis of 71 court cases from 12 countries concluded that in 59 cases access to essential medicines was enforced through the courts as part of the right to health law (Hogerzeil et al. 2006).

This phenomenon has been particularly notable in Latin America, where courts have ordered governments and public authorities to provide treatment for a range of conditions, include new groups of patients in existing packages of benefits, and offer special protection for certain groups, such as people living with HIV/AIDS. In Brazil, over the past decade, courts have reviewed an estimated 100,000 cases concerning whether individuals received medical treatments (mostly medications) to which they were arguably entitled under the terms of the 1988 constitution and the operational guidelines of the national health system. The state of São Paulo alone spent around US$130 million in 2007 to comply with judicial orders (Ferraz 2009). In 2008, the Colombian courts heard more than 142,000 claims regarding health complaints, most of which alleged that health insurers had unfairly denied treatments or medications (Yamin and Parra-Vera 2010) (box 4.2.) In Costa Rica, people have filed a large number of constitutional claims against the social security agency (Wilson 2009), and in Argentina, the courts ordered the state to ensure an uninterrupted supply of antiretroviral drugs to persons with HIV/AIDS.

Countries outside of Latin America also have experienced this "judicialization" in the health sector. A case in South Africa, *Minister of Health v. Treatment Action Campaign*, illustrates a judicial accountability mechanism in action. The bill of rights in the South Africa constitution recognizes the right to health. In August 2001, the Treatment Action Campaign (TAC), a network of organizations and individuals campaigning to increase access to HIV/AIDS treatment, filed a claim before the Pretoria High Court, demanding that the government provide drugs to pregnant women on the grounds that the government had failed to respect the right to life and the right to health. The court decided in favor of TAC and ruled that the government's restrictions were unreasonable. In 2002, the Constitutional Court upheld the Pretoria ruling and confirmed that the policy discriminated against the poor, who could not afford to pay for the medication. It also ruled that health policy should be "reasonable" in development and implementation, meaning that it should be comprehensive, coordinated between levels of government, and focused on those in greatest need.

The role of courts in providing redress in health has raised several concerns. Courts may provide individuals with successful resolutions of their grievances, but courts may also create negative externalities for the health system more generally if they fail to consider the impact of the decisions at the system level. For example, mandating state coverage of medications or services has the potential to be costly and undermine long-term planning and priority setting. Resolving grievances through the court system (90,000 per year in Colombia) may create huge backlogs, politicization, and inefficiency in the sector. Moreover, redress through courts could be regressive if poor and marginalized groups do not have access to the system. Courts can facilitate access through public defenders. NGOs and CSOs also seek to bridge this gap.

Box 4.2

The Court System and Health in Colombia

Both the judicial system and the health system underwent significant reform in Colombia during the early 1990s. The Constitutional Court and the process of judicial complaint, *tutela,* to protect individual and fundamental rights, were introduced in 1991. And in 1993, Law 100 introduced a two-tiered system of health benefits, made up of the contributory regime (Plan Obligatorio de Salud, POS), for those formally employed or earning at least twice the minimum wage, and the subsidized regime (Plan Obligatorio de Salud Subsidiado, POSS), for the poor. The POSS included approximately one-half of the benefits in the contributory regime. Over time, the two regimes were supposed to be merged into one at the POS level of coverage and benefits, thereby providing everyone with an essential health care package.

The strong economic growth of the early 1990s led policy makers to predict that larger numbers of workers would join the formal labor market and start contributing toward the POS, which would increase the resources to provide services. That prediction did not come true, and a large share of the population is still in the informal sector. Approximately 10 percent of the population remains without health coverage, and coverage of the two schemes is unequal. Some essential services are not available for either the population without health insurance or those in the subsidized regimes. The inequalities particularly affect the most vulnerable groups—poor children, large families, and indigenous peoples. The two systems have not merged, although the government is beginning the process. The first step was the provision of the same level of benefits for all children under 18 according to an order of the Constitutional Court of Colombia.

Coverage has increased since 1993, but even today not all the citizens are covered by the POSS, nor have the efficiency and quality gains materialized to the expected extent. Patients have increasingly turned to litigation to secure medications and services not delivered by the system. Approximately 100,000 *tutelas* in health are brought to courts every year, and the majority of them are submitted and provided redress on an individual basis.

In a July 2008 decision, the Constitutional Court upheld the fundamental right to health and access to treatment. The court ordered a restructuring of the health system and the benefits packages and called for the government to unify the POS and POSS for children under 18 before October 2009 and to move toward further unification of the benefit plans for adults, while taking financial sustainability into

(continued next page)

Box 4.2 *(continued)*

account. The decision established a bill of health rights stipulating that the Colombian government must protect all citizens under five circumstances:

- Health services are not delivered because of the patient's inability to pay, including for catastrophic or high-cost procedures.
- Health services are stopped without clear medical reasons.
- Patients do not receive adequate information about their treatment options.
- Patients face unnecessarily burdensome bureaucracy or administrative procedures that might prevent access to services.
- Patients are asked to pay separately for services that are part of an integrated treatment plan.

Since handing down these orders, the Constitutional Court has been assessing whether the government has fully followed them.

Sources: Yamin and Parra-Vera 2010; Authors' interviews.

Education

With the exception of a few examples of GRMs in tertiary education, the literature reviews did not find many examples of formal explicit grievance mechanisms in the education sector, but that result does not mean that people do not complain. The EBRD study found that people do complain about education at a similar rate as for health, and in some countries at an even higher rate. Education is also a common concern among voters in local elections across countries (EBRD 2011).

Few World Bank–supported projects in education incorporate grievance redress, and those that do tend to focus on the allocation of targeted transfers, such as scholarships, rather than providers' accountability. An exception is the Pakistan Sindh Education Sector Project, which includes a complaints management system for three subprograms: the fairness of processes related to teacher recruitment, the disbursement of secondary school stipends for female students, and free textbook distribution to public school students. Complaints are usually received through e-mail, telephone, or letter.

For primary and secondary education, the reason for the low level of formal GRMs may be that grievances and complaints are raised and resolved at the school level. Parents have direct channels to providers in education that do not necessarily exist in the other sectors. Parents can complain to the headmaster of a school or raise a grievance in a parent-teacher meeting. In India, the Sarva Shisksha Abhiyan (Education for All) framework mandates that village education committees receive and handle complaints about irregularities, such as teacher absenteeism and discrimination based on caste or gender, but evidence presented in chapter 3 suggests that parents might not know or care about these committees. Through decentralization and school-based management, parents can have a voice in overall monitoring of school performance, the allocation of school budgets, and teacher hiring and firing.

A review of evaluations of school-based management experiments found that increased decentralization and involvement of parents can have positive effects on the quality of service delivery (Bruns, Filmer, and Patrinos 2011). Decentralized contexts, however, may also pose risks, including the problem of capture if elites dominate local decision making. The poor and excluded groups, such as indigenous peoples and ethnic minorities, may not be empowered or allowed to raise concerns about conditions at the school or the treatment of students. Their exclusion can have serious equity implications and underscores the potential importance of independent and fair channels for parents to express grievances.

Complaints systems in education also start at the facility level in OECD countries. In the United States, the states and school systems often have complaints-handling processes. The New York Department of Education encourages parents to resolve complaints locally. The chancellor of the school system also has set up a formal process for hearing complaints and appeals. The process handles issues under the jurisdiction of the state, and issues related to federal government policies—for example, the No Child Left Behind Act—are referred to a separate channel.[8] Public and private universities generally have independent grievance institutions, such as an ombudsman, to handle complaints from employees, students, and even parents.[9]

Design Issues

In practice, the typical features of a redress system include an information campaign that tells citizens about the functioning of the system and where to complain; dedicated staff or an automated system that logs complaints and monitors resolutions within a timely period; and redress, including remedial actions and potential sanctions. Some have argued that effective systems also monitor and track complaints to improve service delivery and policy and provide feedback to citizens on the outcomes of their complaints (Post and Agarwal 2011; Khan and Giannozzi 2011).

Redress procedures require both credibility and adequate physical or virtual venues where complaints can be received. If people are not convinced that they will get a response, they are unlikely to bother to lodge complaints. Many service users, particularly the most marginalized, may not believe they are entitled to complain.

Physical access is another issue. Redress systems are increasingly providing multiple channels—including offices and opportunities to register complaints via text message and the Internet. Redress procedures that require clients to spend a great deal of time and resources to access them may not work in practice. World Vision's Cash and Food Transfer Pilot Program in Lesotho attempted to decrease travel times by setting up a traveling community help desk, which beneficiaries could use to voice their complaints at the locations where they were to receive cash transfers (Devereux and Mhlanga 2008). Nearly half of the complaints were resolved on the same day that they were lodged. Mexico's Oportunidades program also included a mobile complaints-handling service.

In India, the Rajasthan Health Systems Development project developed a complaints-handling mechanism for members from disadvantaged tribal communities. In a pilot project, staff members from a local organization that worked with the tribal communities were placed in health centers to assist service users in registering their complaints and suggestions. The NGO staff could also help these patients communicate with health center staff members who spoke a different language.

Countries make grievance redress more accessible by providing different venues for lodging complaints. Centrelink, an Australian government agency tasked with the delivery of social benefits, increased awareness of how to complain and provided service users with multiple channels for complaints, including the Internet, telephone, mail, and e-mail. The number of complaints rose 27 percent between 2007 and 2008 (ANAO 2008).

Another example is Uganda's Coalition for Health Promotion and Social Development (HEPS). HEPS is part of the Stop Stock-outs Campaign, an effort that began in response to a finding that less than half of Ugandan public health facilities were stocked with necessary medications, with average stock-outs lasting 2.5 months. HEPS encourages citizens to use text message technology to report stock-out rates to HEPS, which aggregates the information into interactive maps. The maps serve as a tool for informing policy makers and service providers of medicine shortages across the country.

Staffing and Administration

The effectiveness of administrative processes and institutional arrangements for grievance redress also influences the extent to which these systems are used and have an impact. Following the 2002 economic crisis in Argentina, the Ministry of Employment and Labor, with support from the World Bank, set up the cash transfer and public works program, Jefes y Jefas, which included a system for handling complaints and accusations of fraud. In the beginning, the main types of calls coming to a toll-free hotline were requests for information about eligibility, questions about payment dates and delays in payments, and reports of ineligible beneficiaries. The system was quickly overwhelmed. The program was new, some of the rules were unclear, and the call center lacked adequate capacity. The government did not allow staff members to work in shifts, and workers received inadequate training. At peak times, especially when payments were being made, the system was able to respond to only 15 percent of the calls it received, and many individuals were never able to get through to an operator. These problems led to a loss of credibility that undermined confidence in the Jefes program.

In response, the hotline added a system of standard messages to answer frequently asked questions using taped responses, such as dates of payment according to identification numbers, and staffed the call center for 24 hours a day. A standard format for taking accusations of fraud was prepared to ensure that enough information was collected for following up on the claims, and the system was changed so that people could make these complaints through the call center, directly (via e-mail or personally), and through provincial offices of employment and local consultative councils (World Bank 2006).

Colombia's Familias en Acción CCT program is making similar changes to streamline its complaints-handling system. The software that is used to monitor complaints is incorporating a "reply-making assistant" that gives the staff standard templates for responding to common complaints. This change aims to improve response quality and reduce the risk of appeals if responses are insufficient or of poor quality.

These examples underscore the importance of having sufficient staff and adequate systems in place to respond in a timely and effective manner. Some systems also set performance standards and targets, including the average length of time expected to respond to a complaint.[10] The U.K.'s NHS expects primary care practitioners to respond to complaints within 10 working days, and chief executives of NHS organizations are expected to respond within 25 days (NAO 2008a). Colombia's Familias en Acción CCT program stipulates that a complaint related to payments should be filed no more than 10 days after the payment should have been paid, so that it can be resolved during the following payment cycle.

Costs

The more accessible redress procedures are, the more likely they will be effective in strengthening accountability and empowering users. Excessive time spent on redress procedures, however, can increase the costs of service delivery. Balancing accessibility of redress against its potential to reduce efficiency is a design challenge. As a general principle, it is less costly to resolve complaints at the point of service delivery, where information about service practices is clearest and where transaction costs are lowest. Lesotho's traveling help desk managed to resolve nearly half of complaints on the same day they were lodged.

Examples from the United Kingdom also suggest that costs appear to rise substantially when complaints are not resolved at the outset (NAO 2008a, 2008b). The House of Commons Public Administration Select Committee found that systems that resolve complaints early on are relatively cheap (HoC 2008). The story changes when appeals are taken into account. Across the U.K. public sector, internal appeals cost an average of £455 (about US$705) per case, and the costs for independent complaint handlers and for ombudsmen range between £1,500 (about US$2,325) and £2,000 (about US$3,100) (NAO 2005). In adult social care services, the cost of further investigations (both internal and external) was on average £1,960 (about US$3,038) compared to an initial resolution cost of £570 (about US$880). Additional appeal can cost a further £900 (about US$1,395) per case. The NAO concludes that when Department of Welfare and Pensions agencies resolve complaints successfully at the outset, costs may be as much as 40 times cheaper than when complaints are resolved through the appeal process (NAO 2008b).

Summary

Grievance redress mechanisms can serve as important outlets for improving service delivery and holding policy makers and providers accountable. To function effectively, a system of redress requires a well-designed and well-linked supply of redress procedures and organizations that can stimulate and aggregate demand for redress. Technology is becoming more important in collecting, aggregating, and facilitating redress, but it is not a solution on its own. Effective use of technology requires adequate processes, staffing, and resources. Overall, redress procedures are under-developed in many developing countries and deserve further analysis, piloting, and support.

Notes

1. This section draws from background papers by Gauri (2011) and van Stolk (2011).
2. See http://www.dwp.gov.uk/contact-us/complaints-and-appeals/.
3. Hunger Safety Net Programme, "About Us." http://www.hsnp.or.ke/HSNP%20 Web%20index_files/Page382.htm.
4. "French Health System—Complaints." http://www.french-property.com/ guides/france/public-services/health/complaints/.
5. See http://www.mediateur-republique.fr/en-20-citoyen-Contact.
6. National Health Service, "How to Complain," http://www.nhs.uk/ choiceintheNHS/Rightsandpledges/complaints/Pages/NHScomplaints.aspx.
7. The local Patient Advice and Liaison Service office can be found at http:// www.pals.nhs.uk/officemapsearch.aspx.
8. See http://schools.nyc.gov/Offices/OFEA/KeyDocuments/Parent+Complaint+ Procedures.htm.
9. For example, see the Massachussetts Institute of Technology's grievance policies at http://web.mit.edu/policies/ 9/9.6.html.
10. A review of complaints-handling systems in health and social care in a set of European countries found standard times for response to be 1 week for an informal response or acknowledgment of a complaint, 4–5 weeks for a formal review, and 16–52 weeks for an appeal process (Lister et al. 2008). These time periods can be substantially longer for appeals and responses that require an investigation. For example, the New Zealand health commissioner takes 6 to 9 months for a simple investigation, but a complex investigation can take 18 months to 2 years.

References

ANAO (Australian National Audit Office). 2008. "Centrelink's Complaints Handling System." ANAO, Canberra. http://anao.gov.au/~/media/Uploads/ Documents/2008%2009_audit_report_22.pdf.

Bruns, Barbara, Deon Filmer, and Harry Anthony Patrinos. 2011. *Making Schools Work: New Evidence on Accountability Reforms.* Washington, DC: World Bank. http://siteresources.worldbank.org/EDUCATION/Resources/278200-1298568319076/makingschoolswork.pdf.

Devereux, Stephen, and Michael Mhlanga. 2008. "Cash Transfers in Lesotho: An Evaluation of World Vision's Cash and Food Transfers Pilot Project." Brighton, U.K.; Maseru, Lesotho: Centre for Social Protection, Institute for Development Studies, and Mhlanga Consulting Services. http://dgroups.org/file2.axd/e61f4826-0a81-4e80-9b74-5a05a06d3994/Microsoft%20Word%20-%20Lesotho%202008%20-%20CFTTP%20Evaluation%20Report.pdf.

EBRD (European Bank for Reconstruction and Development). 2011. *Life in Transition after the Crisis*. London: European Bank for Reconstruction and Development. http://www.ebrd.com/downloads/research/surveys/LiTS2e_web.pdf.

EBRD and World Bank 2010. "Life in Transition: A Survey of People's Experiences and Attitudes." EBRD, London.

Ferraz, Octavio. 2009. "Right to Health Litigation in Brazil: An Overview of the Research." University of Warwick, School of Law, U.K., May 15. http://papers.ssrn.com/sol3/papers.cfm?abstract_id=1426011.

Fountain, Jane E. 2001. "Paradoxes of Public Sector Customer Service." *Governance* 14 (1): 55–73. http://onlinelibrary.wiley.com/doi/10.1111/0952-1895.00151/pdf.

Gauri, Varun. 2011. "Redressing Grievances and Complaints Regarding Basic Service Delivery." Policy Research Working Paper 5699, World Bank, Washington, DC. http://imagebank.worldbank.org/servlet/WDSContentServer/IW3P/IB/2011/06/22/000158349_20110622085504/Rendered/PDF/WPS5699.pdf.

Gauri, Varun, and Daniel M. Brinks, eds. 2008. *Courting Social Justice: Judicial Enforcement of Social and Economic Rights in the Developing World*. Cambridge, U.K.; New York: Cambridge University Press. http://www.cambridge.org/aus/catalogue/catalogue.asp?isbn=9780521145169&ss=cop.

GAO (General Accountability Office). 2010. "Whistleblower Attention: Sustained Management Attention Needed to Address Long-Standing Program Weaknesses." GAO-10-722 General Accountability Office, Washington, DC. http://www.gao.gov/new.items/d10722.pdf.

Gruenberg, Christian, and Victoria Pereyra Iraola. 2008. "Sistemas de rendición de cuentas. De la teoría promisoria a la práctica concreta: Los casos de México y Argentina." In *Candados y Contrapesos: La Protección de los Programas, Políticas y Derechos Sociales en México y América Latina*, ed. David Gómez-Álvarez, 169–94. Tlaquepaque, Mexico: Instituto Technológico y de Estudios Superiores de Occidente.

HoC (House of Commons). 2008. "When Citizens Complain." Public Administration Select Committee, Fifth Report of Session 2007–08. TSO Publications, London. http://www.publications.parliament.uk/pa/cm200708/cmselect/cmpubadm/409/409.pdf.

Hogerzeil, Hans V., Melanie Samson, Jaume Vidal Casanovas, and Ladan Rahmani-Ocora. 2006. "Is Access to Essential Medicines as Part of the Fulfillment of the Right to Health Enforceable through the Courts?" *Lancet* 368: 305–11. http://www.who.int/medicines/news/Lancet_EssMedHumanRight.pdf.

Khan, Asmeen, and Sara Giannozzi. 2011. "Strengthening the Governance Dimension of Social Safety Nets in ASEAN." Unpublished manuscript, World Bank, Washington, DC. http://siteresources.worldbank.org/SOCIAL PROTECTION/Resources/SP-Discussion-papers/Safety-Nets-DP/1116.pdf.

Lister, Graham, Flemming Rosleff, Markella Boudioni, Fons Dekkers, Elke Jakubowski, and Helen Favelle. 2008. "Handling Complaints in Health and Social Care: International Lessons for England." London: National Audit Office. http://www.nao.org.uk/idoc.ashx?docId=7bc93744-34cb-4f83-8e87-d788bdfcbaf6&version=-1.

Moyer, Mel S. 1984. "Characteristics of Consumer Complainants: Implications for Marketing and Public Policy." *Journal of Public Policy & Marketing* 3: 67–84.

NAO (National Audit Office). 2005. "Citizen Redress: What Citizens Can Do If Things Go Wrong with Public Services." HC 21 Session 2004–2005. http://www.nao.org.uk/publications/0405/citizen_redress.aspx.

———. 2008a. "Feeding Back? Learning from Complaints Handling in Health and Social Care." HC 853 Session 2007–2008. http://www.nao.org.uk/idoc.ashx?docId=3d451e8f-e146-4a60-9b8e-bca59679dc51&version=-1.

———. 2008b. "Department for Work and Pensions: Handling Customer Complaints." HC 995 Session 2007–2008. http://www.nao.org.uk/publications/nao_reports/07-08/0708995.pdf.

Post, David, and Sanjay Agarwal. 2011. "Feedback Matters: Designing Effective Grievance Redress Mechanisms for Bank-Financed Projects." SDV-GAC in Projects: How to Notes, World Bank, Washington, DC. http://siteresources.worldbank.org/EASTASIAPACIFICEXT/Resources/GRMP2-Final.pdf.

Rodriguez Restrepo, Carlos. 2011. "Case Study: Governance in the Colombian Program *Familias en Acción*." Unpublished report.

Silva Villalobos, Verónica, Gastón Blanco, and Lucy Bassett. 2010. "Management Information Systems for Conditional Cash Transfers and Social Protection Systems in Latin America: A Tool for Improved Program Management and Evidence-Based Decision-Making." Social Protection Unit, Human Development Network, World Bank, Washington, DC. http://siteresources.worldbank.org/SAFETYNETSANDTRANSFERS/Resources/mis_ctt_english_full_report.pdf.

van Stolk, Christian. 2011. "Complaints Handling and Service Delivery." Unpublished.

Wilson, Bruce. 2009. "Rights Revolutions in Unlikely Places: The Cases of Colombia and Costa Rica." *Journal of Politics in Latin America* 1 (2): 59–85. http://www.qrmafrica.org/uploads/articles/Wilson1.pdf.

World Bank. 2006. "Project Appraisal Document on a Proposed Loan to the Argentine Republic for a Head of Household Transition Project." World Bank, Washington, DC.

———. 2010. "Philippines: Strengthening the Governance Dimension of the Philippines' Conditional Cash Transfer Program." World Bank, Manila Office, Human and Development and Governance Units.

Yamin, Alicia, and Oscar Parra-Vera. 2010. "Judicial Protection of the Right to Health in Colombia: From Social Demands to Individual claims to Public Debates." *Hastings International and Comparative Law Review* 33 (2):101–29. https://litigation-essentials.lexisnexis.com/webcd/app?action=DocumentDisp lay&crawlid=1&doctype=cite&docid=33+Hastings+Int%27l+%26+Comp.+L .+Rev.+431&srctype=smi&srcid=3B15&key=3a2825fa261735f98b16d595d2 9bcd89.

CHAPTER 5

Summary and Looking Forward

That citizens can contribute to strengthening governance and the quality of service delivery in the human development (HD) sectors through voice and client power is an appealing proposition. There are, however, risks, caveats, and many questions about how this idea works in practice. The relationships among citizens, policy makers, program managers, and service providers are complicated. They are not always direct or easily altered through a single intervention, such as an information campaign or scorecard exercise.

Influencing Service Delivery through Social Accountability

Development projects backed by the World Bank and others in the HD sectors are supporting a diverse set of interventions to inform and motivate citizens to influence service delivery, but most of the mechanisms identified in this book are pilot projects. They include information campaigns, scorecards and report cards, training in financial literacy, and various approaches to grievance redress. Even though many projects are small and experimental, much can be gained from documenting and analyzing them as they are implemented, and much can be learned from other organizations involved in work related to social accountability. This chapter summarizes conclusions and discusses opportunities for further knowledge development.

A number of important messages emerge from the discussion in the previous chapters:

- **Information asymmetries that prevail in the HD sectors can make it difficult for citizens to assess the performance of providers.** Users of services may lack information about service delivery; an understanding of how to interpret information, such as budgets and financial reports; and the capacity to act on such information. A related risk is that people may misunderstand service delivery and act in a way that does not improve its quality or may even undermine it. For example, parents may want to have computers in schools, regardless of whether teachers are trained to use them effectively and support student learning. It is not clear to what extent the provision of information (or what type of information) can remedy these asymmetries. The existing evidence provides room for both optimism and caution.

- **Individually, citizens and users may be reluctant to challenge the authority of providers.** This situation may be the result of unequal power dynamics within a community. People may think they do not have the right or knowledge to question teachers or doctors because of the professionals' status or credentials. People may be concerned about the repercussions of giving negative feedback. Moreover, citizens simply may not have time to give feedback on service delivery by filing a complaint or attending a school meeting. The political and social setting in a country—and the associated power relationships among poor citizens, providers, and the state—may greatly influence the capacity of citizens to use information to hold providers accountable.

- **Individually, social accountability mechanisms may be ineffective.** Passing a right-to-information law does not guarantee that information will be made available to citizens unless information campaigns are undertaken to let people know how to file a request. Similarly, publishing beneficiary lists for a conditional cash transfer (CCT) program is not likely to improve the targeting of a program unless people have access to a hotline or another channel for reporting inaccuracies. Citizens need both information and the channels to use it. It is therefore important to consider how social accountability tools interact with each other.

- **Providers need to be open to the influence of citizens through social accountability mechanisms.** For social accountability mechanisms to influence service delivery, changes are needed in the behavior and the content of the work of frontline service providers. If the incentive framework under which providers operate isolates or protects them from outside pressures—for example, their funding stays the same or they experience no risk of dismissal—social accountability mechanisms, such as scorecards or hotlines, are unlikely to work well. Social accountability is not just a "demand-side" concern. The mechanisms discussed in this book cannot be considered separately from the broader incentive framework under which providers operate.

- **The existence and strength of civil society and an independent media can influence the potential for social accountability mechanisms.** Civil society organizations (CSOs) and the media can facilitate relationships among citizens, policy makers, and providers by furthering access to information and grievance redress. They can disseminate information about how to file a complaint or participate in a social audit or teach citizens how to interpret a budget; they may transform individual attempts to hold providers and policy makers accountable into collective efforts. They can also mobilize support for opening channels for accountability. For example, CSOs in India lobbied for the National Rural Employment Guarantee Act (NREGA) discussed in chapter 3. The interaction between environments of unequal social relations and closed political systems can seriously affect the scope of the mechanisms discussed in this book.

The empirical evidence and operational examples reviewed also suggest practical design questions that influence the transformational role of social accountability mechanisms:

- **Accessibility.** Attention to the accessibility and inclusiveness of social accountability mechanisms is important, particularly in low-income countries and regions. For information interventions and grievance redress, attention to accessibility means designs that take into consideration language, culture, and geographic barriers. For example, to ensure equitable participation, scorecards and social audits should be conducted in locations that can be accessed by a broad segment of the population and at convenient times. Power dynamics at the local level can also influence whether people are likely to participate in a scorecard exercise or to raise a complaint. If a village chief is in charge of a community meeting, poorer, more marginalized citizens and groups may be reluctant to participate or voice their concerns.

- **Data availability and quality.** A simple but critical point about the design of information interventions is that they will not work without good data. Information campaigns about the financing of services and performance can have demanding data requirements. In low- and middle-income countries, data about spending at the facility level may not be easily available. Data on student performance are not collected in some countries, and even where data are available, they may not be accessible at the school level. Scorecard and report card exercises that generate data on performance from subjective assessments of citizens and communities pose different data challenges, including the challenges of collecting good-quality data and the difficulties of interpreting beneficiary assessments (Fiszbein, Ringold, and Rogers 2011).

- **Use of technology.** The use of technology for social accountability has generated considerable excitement. The Stop Stock-outs Campaign in Uganda uses text messaging technology. Grievance redress systems are also using text messages and social media applications to reach citizens. Technology can make information and grievance redress more accessible and potentially easier to use. The design of the user interface is important, as is attention to the administrative systems that support the use of technology. The low-tech hotline for the Jefes cash transfer program in Argentina is an example of a tool that was first introduced without adequate systems and human capacity in place to run smoothly.

Incorporating Social Accountability into Human Development Projects

The discussion so far points to some considerations for the use of social accountability mechanisms within development programs, including those supported by the World Bank, other donors, and CSOs. Basic questions include which instruments to choose, when to use them, and how to assess whether they work.

First, what can social accountability bring to the project? The first matter to settle is what kind of problem the project is trying to address. If the project is supporting a new program or substantial changes in the rules of an existing program, an information campaign that informs people about their rights would make sense. If weak management of public funds or corruption is an issue, information interventions that publicize the amount of school grants or discussions among citizens, program managers, and providers through a scorecard or social audit may be an option for improving transparency and identifying leakages of funds.

Grievance redress could contribute to managing inclusion and exclusion errors in targeted programs across the HD sectors, both at the individual level (cash benefits, scholarships) and at the institutional level (grants to schools or clinics) by giving citizens a channel for reporting error, fraud, and corruption. Table 5.1 lists some potential problems that could conceivably be addressed through information campaigns, scorecards, social audits, and grievance redress.

Second, what is the country context? A related question is whether a social accountability intervention is appropriate in a particular context. A scorecard of public sector schools or health facilities will be of limited

Table 5.1   Social Accountability in HD Projects: Some Examples

Tool	Problem	Type of approach	Ingredients
Information campaigns	Low awareness of the availability of services and benefits Lack of awareness about performance of services Corruption, fraud, weak financial management Weak accountability of providers (absenteeism, poor quality)	Campaigns through the newspaper, radio, and other media Public expenditure tracking survey Budget literacy training	Quality data A communications strategy, especially to reach excluded groups Program and project staff Independent media and CSOs
Scorecards and social audits	Corruption, fraud, weak financial management Weak accountability of providers (absenteeism, poor quality)	Scorecards for HD service delivery Social audits of public works programs	Technical assistance to design, execute, and analyze surveys of beneficiaries, providers, and facilities Facilitators to manage face-to-face meetings Cooperation and ownership from providers and program managers Independent media and CSOs to disseminate findings Monitoring and follow-up mechanisms to ensure that the action plan is implemented

(continued next page)

Table 5.1   *(continued)*

Tool	Problem	Type of approach	Ingredients
Grievance redress mechanisms (program level)	Targeting of errors Provider malpractice Poor conditions of facilities Absenteeism Corruption and fraud Services that do not meet performance standards Fees charged for services that should be free	Hotlines Complaints boxes at facilities E-mail and text message feedback lines Help desks Mobile complaints units	Accessible and credible grievance channels An information campaign to inform the public Civil society to assist citizens with filing complaints A system for logging and responding to complaints Staff in place to field and respond to complaints Processes for redress and sanctions Monitoring systems to ensure that complaints are responded to and aggregated to inform policy Performance standards (time expected to receive a response)

Sources: Aiyar et al. 2009; authors.

value if most of the community uses private services, but a report card may be useful for informing citizens about the relative quality of providers in their area. Political economy and the political and institutional contexts also deserve consideration, including whether a developed civil society and independent media exist to enable the use of access to information and grievance redress.

Third, do preconditions exist to support implementation? At the most basic level, it is fundamental to consider whether the government is interested in the program, wants it, and will assume ownership of it. If not, implementation may be slow and require additional technical assistance and support. Availability of data (and the ability to generate data) is another important precondition. A final consideration is whether the resources to properly staff and manage the social accountability mechanisms are in place. Social audits and scorecards rely on CSOs for implementation and on local government officials or program officers to facilitate relationships between citizens and providers and to monitor follow-up actions. Grievance redress mechanisms (GRMs) require a staff to handle complaints and the systems for monitoring and follow-up. A minimum capacity in these areas can also be considered an important precondition for success.

Fourth, what will ensure sustainability of the effort? Attention to political, technical, and financial sustainability can influence the success or failure of a social accountability mechanism. A challenge is to identify what happens when the project ends:

- **Political sustainability.** Governments may view as threatening the efforts to challenge the authority of providers, such as through a scorecard or a social audit. Such undertakings therefore require management of the political and social conflict they may generate. More generally, when social accountability instruments are new and experimental, their political sustainability requires efforts to build a constituency and capacity for implementation among the government officials, civil society, and donors involved.

- **Operational sustainability.** Information interventions such as scorecards and report cards often tend to be one-time exercises, financed by donor projects that are typically not repeated. Follow-up processes and oversight are important to ensure that the action items defined during a scorecard exercise are actually implemented in practice and that plans are in place to repeat the process to track progress over time.

- **Financial sustainability.** Long-term planning can ensure that activities are sustained over time and incorporated into recurrent budgets at the sector and program level. For exercises such as information interventions, the planning would include staff time to follow up, monitor results, and assess whether it would be useful to repeat the effort. For GRMs built into programs or sectors, financial sustainability means a commitment to fund and staff the system on an ongoing basis.

Fifth, what about monitoring and evaluation? Attention to monitoring and evaluation during the design phase through to the conclusion of the project is critical to know whether it succeeded. Given the experimental nature of many of these projects, building in opportunities for learning through evaluation can pay off. Questions during the design phase include the following: What are the performance indicators? Is there ongoing monitoring through administrative or survey data? And is there an evaluation?

Implications for Future Work

The evidence base on social accountability mechanisms in the HD sectors is under development. A small but growing set of evaluations—mainly in the education sector—tests the impact of information interventions on service delivery and HD outcomes, leaving ample space for future experiments to test how to make social accountability work at the country level.

First, more empirical evidence is needed. At the sector level, social protection and health in particular could benefit from greater attention. The potential exists to build knowledge around the use of active information interventions such as scorecards and grievance redress mechanisms. Much can be gained from documenting, analyzing, and learning from the growing body of experience with social accountability in the HD sectors, and HD projects have the potential to serve as a laboratory of experimentation with social accountability interventions. Evaluating and documenting these experiences can help to improve the use of these tools in the future.

Second, investment in better quality evidence is needed. Evaluations of social accountability measures are by nature complex. Social accountability efforts are frequently introduced alongside other service delivery reforms—including the introduction of new programs and services, such as a grievance redress measure along with a CCT program—and it is not necessarily straightforward to disentangle their impact from other changes. In addition, social accountability measures tend to be small pilots, making it a challenge to ensure adequate sample sizes to detect statistically meaningful effects and determine when something is truly not working (Andrews 1989). The potential exists to improve quality through upstream attention to the quality of evaluation design (see appendix 1).

The good news is that the evidence base is set to grow with the forthcoming evaluations of information interventions within the context of World Bank projects. These projects are testing, among other issues, the effectiveness of different types of information campaigns in Indonesia, complaints-handling for a CCT program in Panama, and scorecards in health and education in the Arab Republic of Egypt and Nepal.

In addition to impact evaluations, social accountability interventions require more long-term monitoring through ongoing efforts to measure service delivery and its outcomes through administrative data and surveys. Monitoring changes in the performance of services is particularly important because the link between information and redress measures and HD outcomes may not be direct or immediate. Some of the initiatives, such as scorecards, may be one-off interventions, and others, such as grievance redress mechanisms, may be ongoing elements of a program. Intermediate indicators of service delivery, such as provider absenteeism in health and education, leakage rates, and targeting of errors, can be used to monitor governance and service delivery (Fiszbein, Ringold, and Rogers 2011).

Third, more concrete operational guidance is needed on the "how-to" of implementing social accountability interventions in the HD sectors. Alongside impact evaluation and performance monitoring, process evaluations and other forms of assessment can be helpful for understanding what works in implementation. Design features and implementation are critical to the success of social accountability interventions, and that success can be captured by documenting the experiences of citizens, providers, donors, and other participants.

References

Aiyar, Yamimi, Bala Posani, Abhijit Patnaik, and Mandakini Devasher. 2009. "Institutionalizing Social Accountability: Considerations for Policy." Working Paper 2, Accountability Initiative, Centre for Policy Research, New Delhi. http://indiagovernance.gov.in/download.php?filename=files/Accountability .pdf.

Andrews, Donald W. K. 1989. "Power in Econometric Applications." *Econometrica* 57 (5): 1059–90. http://cowles.econ.yale.edu/P/cp/p07a/p0737.pdf.

Fiszbein, Ariel, Dena Ringold, and Halsey Rogers. 2011. "Making Services Work: Indicators, Assessments, and Benchmarking of the Quality and Governance of Public Service Delivery in the Human Development Sectors." Working Paper 5690, World Bank, Washington, DC. http://imagebank.worldbank.org/servlet/WDSContentServer/IW3P/IB/2011/06/20/000158349_20110620083658/Rendered/PDF/WPS5690.pdf.

How Can Evidence on Social Accountability Interventions Be Improved?

A central message emerging from this book is that there is ample scope to expand the body of empirical evidence on social accountability in the human development sectors. Why then has this area proven so challenging for researchers? This appendix discusses some of the reasons and suggests some practical ways evaluations and analysis can be improved.

Simultaneity of Interventions

Some of the evidence on information campaigns, report cards, and scorecards comes from interventions that had multiple components. The information campaign might have been accompanied by training; focus group discussions among providers; or motivation, mobilization, and coordination by a nongovernmental organization (NGO) or an outside organization. In these cases, it is very difficult—and often impossible—to isolate the effects of the intervention's individual components and determine which elements contributed to success and which had no impact or even worsened outcomes. Should the intervention be exported wholesale to other contexts for testing, or should we test only the components that the implementers or evaluators believed (but not estimated) were the most effective? How do we know what exactly happened?

Take, for example, the successful information intervention in Uganda that both improved health outcomes and altered provider behavior (Björkman and Svensson 2008). First, it is not clear which intervention component was most responsible for the results: the report card, the information about rights and entitlements, the community encouragement to identify problems and necessary changes in provider behavior in a community action plan, the private meeting with providers that demonstrated how their perceptions of quality differed from household assessments, or the meeting in which the community and providers agreed on a community contract. Second, interpreting what exactly happened is also a bit of a challenge. Although the results are consistent with an improvement in provider accountability, they are also consistent with a pure stimulus to demand and an increase in the intrinsic motivation of providers who might have been receiving feedback on their performance for the first time.

In contrast, in the Indonesian cash transfer experiment, many intervention components were experimentally allocated to different areas. When inviting community members to rank households from richest to poorest, the designers of the program also randomized whether or not village elites were invited to the meeting and the explicit form of the ranking, among other things (Alatas et al. 2011). Because different areas had different combinations of the intervention components, and because these variants had been randomized across areas, comparing areas with different combinations allows us to learn which individual component added any value. Sometimes variants occurred at the level of the meeting so that half of a village's meetings were conducted in one way and the other half in another, which generated variation. Similarly, the intervention in Kenya in which parents were trained to monitor and evaluate their children's teachers had been experimentally cross-cut with other interventions designed to measure the effectiveness of contract teachers and a system of tracking students by their achievement levels (Duflo, Dupas, and Kremer 2009). Combining the interventions allowed us to learn about the impact of these individual components and their combinations (for more on cross-cutting interventions, see Duflo, Glennerster, and Kremer 2006).

Another perhaps less expensive and less complicated method for learning about what actually happened involves forming hypotheses about which outcomes should be affected if a certain component is relevant and which outcomes should not be affected. The radio programs in Benin could have served simply as a demand stimulus, or they could have motivated listeners to demand that their schools make proper use of the new education grants they were receiving. To distinguish between these two mechanisms, however, the authors of the study measured both (1) household investments and policy awareness and (2) investments made by the school (Keefer and Khemani 2011). Because people exposed to the health and education radio programs were not any more aware of school policies, and because the schools did not alter their investments, we can reasonably doubt that the information received by households improved provider accountability. Instead, the radio programs more likely increased the demand for education services, which in turn improved children's literacy.

(Lack of) Representativeness of Sample

One of the risks of information interventions, and those that require the participation of clients identified in this book, is elite capture, meaning that only the wealthiest or the most interested and engaged members of a community participate in intervention activities rather than the poor and other vulnerable groups such as women and minorities. If these participants then form the evaluation sample and we are concerned with individual outcomes (Did you file a complaint? Were you charged the posted amount in the clinic?), we could be estimating the impact of the intervention for this particular type of person, rather than for someone representative of the village. It is unclear whether such a sample would lead to over- or underestimates of program impact. If active members of the community are more likely to translate the information or training received during the intervention into action, our evaluation results would overestimate impact. If, however, these participants stand to gain the least (perhaps because they have other means of pressuring service providers, they have checked out of the public sector, or their very demeanor lessens the chance of an under-the-table payment), we could underestimate the potential of the intervention in our evaluation. Thus, the *cross-sectional* representativeness of the sample determines how much we can learn about an intervention's impact on the average targeted beneficiary of public services.

The *intertemporal* representativeness of the sample would presumably matter as well. If we measure awareness or outcomes related to how users interact with service providers immediately after an information or training intervention, we might see informed and empowered users. The end-line surveys of the evaluations that we have highlighted generally take place between 2 and 12 months after the interventions. Were we to measure the same outcomes two or three years later, would the results persist? Do we think that a one-time intervention, often not lasting more than seven days, would permanently alter the trajectory of user-provider relations in an area? In the Kenyan intervention that trained parents to monitor and evaluate their children's teachers, the researchers returned to measure outcomes one year after the program ended and found that the positive effect of this intervention on learning outcomes had worn off (Duflo et al. 2007). The impact of school report cards persisted in rural Pakistan two years after the initial distribution of report cards (Andrabi, Das, and Ijaz Khwaja 2009), although it can be argued that because report cards were distributed a second time, parents continued to respond to the information and would have pressured schools if they did not see improvements.

The fixes for these problems of cross-sectional and intertemporal representativeness are relatively straightforward. Implementers of information campaigns or more participatory interventions and survey firms that measure outcomes can be provided with an explicit sampling strategy that aims for representativeness, so that they do not have to depend on local village leaders to find people. Longer follow-up surveys—one to two years after the intervention has ended—can also provide evidence on the sustainability of these types of interventions.

Nature of the Indicators: Self-Reported versus Objective

If we are interested in empowering households to choose or demand better health care, which would be more convincing evidence that we have been successful: (A) self-reported data from households whose members tell us that they feel comfortable asking their providers questions, they know all their rights and the rules applicable to providers, and they have filed a complaint, or (B) direct observations of patient-provider interactions in clinics where providers adhere more closely to medical guidelines, patients ask more questions, and a log of complaints is sent to the relevant authority?

Although it is easier to collect the information required for (A), the information in (B) is more objective in the sense that data collected in this fashion will not suffer from a number of biases prone to self-reports. First, the researcher will not encounter courtesy bias, which could arise if households feel obliged to say that they have filed a complaint when they have attended motivation sessions that urged them to be more active. Second, the data collected under (B) would be measuring human development outcomes more directly (actual quality of medical advice received in clinics), rather than the intermediate outcomes that we have *posited* as instrumental for improving human development outcomes (knowledge of rules and rights that *could* make households demand better services). Third, individuals typically recall their interactions with providers with a large degree of error and tend to focus on aspects of interactions that may not be related to technical efficacy (Lundberg 2008; Deichmann and Lall 2003).

Often, however, it is not difficult to find objective measures of impact. Although it was not an impact evaluation, one study measured outcomes before and after social audits of India's National Rural Employment Guarantee Scheme in the state of Andhra Pradesh (Aiyar and Samji 2009). Workers' knowledge and awareness of the scheme increased dramatically, but the more convincing evidence that the program had an impact comes from improvements in the amenities available at worksites, such as the availability of drinking water, first aid kits, and facilities for shade. In two experiments in Indonesia, researchers measured the number of complaint forms stuffed in the complaint boxes (Alatas et al. 2011) and the number of problems voiced during village meetings (Olken 2007).

Low Statistical Power and Type II Errors

Determining if an intervention has worked often comes down to statistics. In particular, it comes down to a hypothesis test to see if the patterns in the data allow us to reject something called the *null hypothesis*. Under the null hypothesis, the program had no real impact, and any difference that we estimate between those with the program and those without the program has arisen by pure chance. What typically allows us to *reject* the null hypothesis is a comparison of the estimated program impact to the estimated standard error of that impact. If that ratio is larger than 1.96, we say that we can reject the null hypothesis of no impact with a confidence level of 95 percent or that our estimated impact is statistically significant at the 5 percent level. This means that if we repeated the experiment 100 times, we would commit a Type I error only 5 percent of the time and falsely think that the program worked when it really did not.

What about the converse—when our ratio of estimated impact to estimated standard error is less than 1.96 and we *fail to reject* the null hypothesis? Does this mean that we can *accept* the null hypothesis that the program had no impact? Unfortunately, we often cannot, and instead

we need to worry about the possibility of committing a Type II error—
that is, estimating that the program had no impact when it really did.
When the likelihood of making this type of error is high, we say that our
hypothesis test has low statistical power.

Say, for example, we implement an information campaign that
increases school attendance by an average of 30 percentage points from a
baseline attendance rate of 50 percent, and say that this average improvement is estimated with a standard error of 20 percentage points. This
impact is certainly not statistically significant, but would we feel entirely
comfortable inferring that the information campaign had no impact?
Clearly not. Instead, this result is different from estimating an impact of
0.68 percentage points with an estimated standard error of 0.30 percentage points. In the first case, our data do not have the precision for concluding whether the intervention worked, for we cannot statistically distinguish
a rather large effect from zero. In the second case, we have estimated an
impact of less than 1 percentage point, and our standard error suggests
that this is a very precisely estimated impact of zero.

Small sample sizes or noisy data can often lead us into situations in
which we estimate *economically* significant program impacts that are
not *statistically* significant. How do we know if this has occurred? How
do we know when to doubt a conclusion that a certain program has not
worked? Andrews (1989) provides some guidance and proposes *inverse
power calculations*. These calculations yield the number below which
the true impact would have a less than equal chance of being detected
and which would make a coin toss a better predictor of program effectiveness than the data. This number is easy to calculate from most
impact evaluation studies and typically involves simply multiplying the
estimated standard error associated with program impact by 1.96. From
the example—school attendance increases by 30 percentage points in
response to an information campaign—we can see that if the true
impact of the program were anywhere between 0 and 39.2 percentage
points, we would be better off flipping a coin (heads, the program
worked; tails, it did not) than relying on our data to estimate whether
the program had an impact.

If one has a slightly obsessive-compulsive personality and takes the
time to trawl through the tables of results, one would see that many of
the impact evaluations we have presented suffer from low statistical
power. The imprecisely estimated impacts of zero in these studies often
cannot be statistically distinguished from impacts that we would consider
quite large (and that we would publicize had the standard errors been

smaller). Thus, we often cannot tell if we need better interventions or just better evaluations.

Design versus Substance

The success of information campaigns and mobilization interventions would also presumably depend on the quality of the implementers. If the messenger is condescending or uninspiring, he or she may fail to deliver the message even if the target audience would have been receptive to it and may even have acted upon it. Similarly, an intervention may be flawed because it is perceived as time-consuming or burdensome for participants. These issues are all related to the design of an intervention (how it is implemented) rather than the substance of intervention (what is being implemented). In many of the evaluations reviewed here, we learn about the effectiveness of the design and substance together, not separately. Thus, if an intervention flops, we do not know if it was a promising idea but needed a better design or if the intervention itself is truly an ineffective method for improving human development outcomes.

We have presented evidence that program design could matter for improving human development outcomes. The national HIV/AIDS curriculum implemented by teachers in rural Kenya had no impact on teenage childbearing, whereas in the same area, an NGO-implemented information campaign about the HIV risks associated with older men did decrease pregnancies (Duflo, Glennester, and Kremer 2006; Dupas 2011). Among HIV/AIDS patients in Kenya, medicine adherence was higher with weekly rather than daily text message reminders (Pop-Eleches et al. 2011). In Indonesia, community members seemed to get tired or distracted toward the end of meetings when they were asked to rank households by wealth in a community-based targeting intervention (Alatas et al. 2011).

Evidence from the financial literature makes this point more strongly and suggests that features of a program that we might not consider important in decision making are sometimes as important in determining final outcomes as the standard features that we tend to tinker with. In South Africa, researchers experimented with interest rates and the content of loan advertisements that were mailed to former clients of a consumer lender. They found that reducing the number of example loans displayed on the ad, avoiding any mention of what could be done with the loan, and including a photo of an attractive woman increased loan take-up as much as a 25 percent or 200 basis point reduction in the interest rate (Bertrand et al. 2009).

How Can We Generate Useful Evidence?

Although the five problems we discussed are common to many evaluations, they are relatively easy to overcome. Table A1.1 summarizes potential solutions and examples of studies that have used them and resources
for more information.

Table A1.1   Summary of Resources for Improving Evaluations

Problem	Potential solutions	Resources
Low statistical power	Ensure adequate sample size. Intervene in smaller units (villages rather than districts, or clinics rather than villages). Use a data collection protocol that stresses quality rather than speed.	Gertler et al. 2011 Duflo, Glennerster, and Kremer 2006
Simultaneity of interventions	Cross-cut interventions so that one group gets intervention A, another gets intervention B, and another gets the combination of A and B. Generate hypotheses about which types of outcomes should be affected by a particular intervention component and which should not, and measure both sets of outcomes. For example, if an information campaign improved teacher accountability, we should see differences in teacher behavior, not just improvements in final test scores.	Olken 2007 Alatas et al. 2011 Duflo, Dupas, and Kremer 2009 Keefer and Khemani 2011 Duflo, Glennerster, and Kremer 2006
(Lack of) representativeness of sample	For cross-sectional representativeness: specify that survey firm NGO or civil society organization must randomly sample households or individuals within geographic units to participate in intervention activities and to be surveyed. For intertemporal representativeness: specify that endline survey must occur at least 12 months after intervention.	Hastings and Weinstein 2008 Björkman and Svensson 2008 Duflo et al. 2007 Andrabi, Das, and Ijaz Khwaja 2009
Nature of the indicators: self-reported versus objective	Measure objective correlates of all self-reported data. Measure outcomes through direct observations in clinics, schools, village meetings, employment offices, or worksites.	Alatas et al. 2011 Das and Hammer 2007 Muralidharan and Sundararaman 2010 Fiszbein, Ringold, and Rogers 2011
Design versus substance	Build implementation features into the evaluation design. Collect data on users' perceptions of the implementers.	Olken 2007 Alatas et al. 2011 Bertrand et al. 2009 Pop-Eleches et al. 2011

Source: Authors.

References

Aiyar, Yamini, and Salimah Samji. 2009. "Transparency and Accountability in NREGA: A Case Study of Andhra Pradesh." Working Paper 1, Accountability Initiative, Centre for Policy Research, New Delhi. http://indiagovernance.gov .in/download.php?filename=files/31_1244199489.pdf.

Alatas, Vivi, Abhijit Banerjee, Rema Hanna, Benjamin A. Olken, and Julia Tobias. 2011. "Targeting the Poor: Evidence from a Field Experiment in Indonesia." NBER Working Paper 15980, National Bureau of Economic Research, Cambridge, MA. http://www.nber.org/papers/w15980.pdf.

Andrabi, Tahir, Jishnu Das, and Asim Ijaz Khwaja. 2009. "Report Cards: The Impact of Providing School and Child Test-Scores on Educational Markets." Unpublished manuscript, Department of Economics, Harvard University. http://www.hks.harvard.edu/fs/akhwaja/papers/RC_08Oct09Full.pdf.

Andrews, Donald W. K. 1989. "Power in Econometric Applications." *Econometrica* 57 (5): 1059–90. http://cowles.econ.yale.edu/P/cp/p07a/p0737.pdf.

Bertrand, Marianne, Dean Karlan, Sendhil Mullainathan, Eldar Shafir, and Jonathan Zinman. 2009. "What's Advertising Content Worth? Evidence from a Consumer Credit Marketing Experiment." Unpublished manuscript, Yale University. http://papers.ssrn.com/sol3/papers.cfm?abstract_id=1532213.

Björkman, Martina, and Jakob Svensson. 2008. "Power to the People: Evidence from a Randomized Field Experiment of a Community-Based Monitoring Project." *Quarterly Journal of Economics* 124 (2): 735–69. http://qje.oxford journals.org/content/124/2/735.full.pdf+html.

Das, Jishnu, and Jeffrey Hammer. 2007. "Location, Location, Location: Residence, Wealth and the Quality of Medical Care in Delhi, India." *Health Affairs* 26 (3): w338–51. http://content.healthaffairs.org/content/26/3/w338.full.pdf+ html.

Deichmann, Uwe, and Somil V. Lall. 2003. "Are You Satisfied? Citizen Feedback and Delivery of Urban Services." Working Paper 3070, World Bank, Washington, DC. http://imagebank.worldbank.org/servlet/WDSContent Server/IW3P/IB/2003/07/08/000094946_03062004020023/Rendered/ PDF/multi0page.pdf.

Duflo, Esther, Pascaline Dupas, and Michael Kremer. 2009. "Additional Resources versus Organizational Changes in Education: Experimental Evidence from Kenya." Unpublished manuscript, Department of Economics, Massachusetts Institute of Technology. http://econ-www.mit.edu/files/4286.

Duflo, Esther, Pascaline Dupas, Michael Kremer, and Samuel Sinei. 2007. "Education and HIV/AIDS Prevention: Evidence from a Randomized Evaluation in Western Kenya." Working Paper 4024, World Bank, Washington, DC. http:// imagebank.worldbank.org/servlet/WDSContentServer/IW3P/IB/2006/10/04/ 000016406_20061004093411/Rendered/PDF/wps4024.pdf.

Duflo, Esther, Rachel Glennerster, and Michael Kremer. 2006. "Using Randomization in Development Economics Research: A Toolkit." Technical Working Paper 333, National Bureau of Economic Research, Cambridge, MA. http://www.nber.org/papers/t0333.pdf.

Dupas, Pascaline. 2011. "Do Teenagers Respond to HIV Risk Information? Evidence from a Field Experiment in Kenya." *American Economic Journal: Applied Economics* 3 (1): 1–34. http://pubs.aeaweb.org/doi/pdfplus/10.1257/app.3.1.1.

Fiszbein, Ariel, Dena Ringold, and Halsey Rogers. 2011. "Making Services Work: Indicators, Assessments, and Benchmarking of the Quality and Governance of Public Service Delivery in the Human Development Sectors." Working Paper 5690, World Bank, Washington, DC. http://imagebank.worldbank.org/servlet/WDSContentServer/IW3P/IB/2011/06/20/000158349_20110620083658/Rendered/PDF/WPS5690.pdf.

Gertler, Paul J., Sebastian Martinez, Patrick Premand, Laura B. Rawlings, and Christel M. J. Vermeersch. 2011. *Impact Evaluation in Practice*. Washington, DC: World Bank. http://siteresources.worldbank.org/EXTHDOFFICE/Resources/5485726-1295455628620/Impact_Evaluation_in_Practice.pdf.

Hastings, Justine S., and Jeffrey M. Weinstein. 2008. "Information, School Choice, and Academic Achievement: Evidence from Two Experiments." *Quarterly Journal of Economics* 123 (4): 1373–414. http://qje.oxfordjournals.org/content/123/4/1373.full.pdf+html.

Keefer, Philip, and Stuti Khemani. 2011. "Mass Media and Public Services: The Effects of Radio Access on Public Education in Benin." Policy Research Working Paper 5559, World Bank, Washington, DC. http://www-wds.worldbank.org/servlet/WDSContentServer/WDSP/IB/2011/02/07/000158349_20110207095259/Rendered/PDF/WPS5559.pdf.

Lundberg, Mattias. 2008. "Client Satisfaction and Perceived Quality of Primary Health Care in Uganda." In *Are You Being Served: New Tools for Measuring Service Delivery*, ed. Samia Amin, Jishnu Das, and Markus Goldstein, 313–41. Washington, DC: World Bank. http://www-wds.worldbank.org/external/default/WDSContentServer/WDSP/IB/2008/02/15/000333038_20080215064605/Rendered/PDF/424820PUB0ISBN1LIC0disclosed0Feb131.pdf.

Muralidharan, Karthik, and Venkatesh Sundararaman. 2010. "Contract Teachers: Experimental Evidence from India." Unpublished manuscript, University of California, San Diego. http://www.isid.ac.in/~pu/conference/dec_10_conf/Papers/KarthikMuralidharan.pdf.

Olken, Benjamin A. 2007. "Monitoring Corruption: Evidence from a Field Experiment in Indonesia." *Journal of Political Economy* 115 (2): 200–49. http://econ-www.mit.edu/files/2913.

Pop-Eleches, Cristian, Harsha Thirumurthy, James P. Habyarimana, Joshua G. Zivin, Markus P. Goldstein, Damien De Walque, Leslie Mackeen, Jessica Haberer, Sylvester Kimaiyo, John Sidle, Duncan Ngare, and David R. Bangsberg. 2011. "Mobile Phone Technologies Improve Adherence to Antiretroviral Treatment in a Resource Limited Setting: A Randomized Controlled Trial of Text Message Reminders." *AIDS* 25 (6): 825–34. http://journals.lww.com/aidsonline/Abstract/2011/03270/Mobile_phone_technologies_improve_adherence_to.13.aspx.

Portfolio Review Methodology

In an effort to capture the use of social accountability tools in human development (HD) sector projects, this study included a review of World Bank project appraisal documents (PADs) and other program documents of 427 HD projects that went to the Board between FY2005 and FY2010. The sample included 130 projects in the health, nutrition, and population sector; 132 in education; and 91 in social protection. Sonar Professional, a text-mining software, was used to search documents for key words (box A2.1). In addition to the specific key words used, the software also searched for combinations; that is, the software identified 1 key word occurring within 10 words of another. For example, the software allowed for a search for the term *accountability*, occurring within 10 words from the word *community*. The key words included 30 terms that were related to the theme of social accountability. This process identified 380 projects that included at least one of the key words.

Following this first round of search for key words in project documents, another software, ATLAS TI, was used to identify passages and paragraphs of documents that contained substantial references to the use of social accountability or demand-side accountability measures. The ATLAS TI software helped us identify passages in the PADs and program documents that described in detail the proposed accountability

---

Box A2.1

Key Words

agency, beneficiary, citizen rights, citizen voice, civil society organization, community-based organization, community mobilization, community monitoring, complaints handling, corruption, decentralization, demand-side accountability, elite capture, empowerment, end-user survey, freedom of information, grievance and redress, information campaign, local governance, parent-teacher organization, participation, participatory budgeting, perception survey, report cards, right to information, school-based management, scorecard, social accountability, social audit, service delivery accountability, user satisfaction.

Source: Authors.

---

component to be implemented through the project. Using this tool, we included all projects that had either a transparency and accountability component attached to them or a monitoring component that also included citizen monitoring to increase accountability of providers. All PADs that produced at least six key word hits from the first round were used in the second round search, which resulted in 235 PADs. Using ATLAS TI, we identified 36 projects that included social accountability measures in their project design. These projects are listed in table A2.1.

The PAD review indicated only proposed inclusion of accountability measures in World Bank projects. Because many projects had already been implemented or were in the process of being implemented, we also reviewed project implementation completion reports and implementation status reports to assess if the components specified in the project documents were implemented as proposed.

In addition to these reports, we requested the team leaders of the 36 identified projects to answer a brief survey consisting of eight questions related to the specific components referenced in the PADs. The questions focused on the status of implementation of accountability measures in the project, measures for process or impact evaluation, and the sustainability and scalability of the accountability measures.

The review process was complemented by a survey of HD teams across the World Bank to find any projects that were not captured through the formal PAD review process. This survey was conducted in

Table A2.1   HD Projects That Include Social Accountability in Their Design, FY2005–FY2010

Health	Education	Social protection
Bangladesh Health, Nutrition, and Population Sector Program (information campaign)	India Second Elementary Education Project (information campaign)	Angola Local Development Project (scorecards)
Bolivia Social Sector Programmatic DPC II (information campaign, citizen report cards)	Indonesia School Operational Assistance-Knowledge Improvement for Transparency and Accountability Project (BOS-KITA) (information campaign, complaints-handling system)	Bolivia Investing in Youth and Children Project (social audit, complaints-handling system)
Eritrea HIV/AIDS, Sexually Transmitted Infections, Tuberculosis, Malaria, Reproductive Health Project (information campaign)	Kenya Education Sector Project (information campaign)	Dominican Republic Performance and Accountability of Social Sector DPL I (information campaign, scorecards)
Ethiopia Protection of Basic Services Project (information campaign, scorecards)	Nepal Education for All Project (social audit)	Dominican Republic Social Protection Project (social audit)
Guatemala Maternal, Child Health and Nutrition Project (social audit)	Pakistan Sindh Education Sector Project (information campaign, complaints-handling system)	Ethiopia Protection of Basic Services Project (scorecards, citizen report cards)
Indonesia Early Childhood Development and Education Project (information campaign, complaints-handling system)	Senegal Education for All Project (information campaign, scorecards)	Kenya Youth Empowerment Project (social audit, complaints-handling system)
Kenya Total War against AIDS Project (information campaign)		Malawi Social Action Fund (scorecards)
Kyrgyz Republic Health and Social Protection Project (information campaign, complaints-handling system)		Nigeria Community and Social Development Project (information campaign)

(continued next page)

Table A2.1   *(continued)*

Health	Education	Social protection
Madagascar Sustainable Health Systems Project (scorecards, information campaign)		Pakistan Social Safety Net TA (information campaign, complaints-handling system)
Maldives Integrated Development Project (scorecards, citizen report cards)		Panama Support to the Red de Oportunidades Project (information campaign, complaints-handling system)
Nepal Second HIV/AIDS Project (scorecards)		Romania Social Inclusion Project (information campaign)
Nepal Health Sector Program (scorecards)		Rwanda Second Community Living Standards Grant (complaints-handling system)
Nicaragua Health Services Extension and Modernization Project (social audits)		Second Northern Uganda Social Action Fund (scorecards, citizen report cards) Tanzania Second Social Action Fund (scorecards, citizen report cards)

Source: Authors, based on review of PADS.

December 2010–January 2011 and asked team members to list projects that had citizen participation, monitoring, or transparency components attached to them; their implementation process in terms of process evaluations and reviews; challenges they faced in implementation, and resources required.

Summary of Impact Evaluations

Sector	Nature of intervention	Length of intervention	Time between start of intervention and end line survey	Main results	Sample size	Evaluation strategy	Evaluation author(s)
INFORMATION CAMPAIGNS							
Benin — Education	Education and health-related programming on community radio stations.	Constant	No temporal element; identification of impact comes from spatial variation.	No significant increase in quantity of education inputs; one s.d increase in community radio access increases literacy by 8 percentage points. Households that listen to community radio purchase books for additional 1.8 children.	32 communes, 210 villages, 210 schools, 4,000 households, 2,100 children	Natural experiment + commune fixed effects.	Keefer and Khemani 2011
Bolivia, Peru, and the Philippines — Social protection	SMS or letter reminders about savings among saving account holders until they reach saving goal. Treatment variant includes salience of saving goal (for example, photo of saving goal).	Monthly reminders throughout account holder's goal term	3 to 24 months	Reminders increased saving. Effectiveness of reminder higher when saving goal made salient.	9,652 (Bolivia) 2,968 (Peru) 1,547 (Philippines)	RCT: Individual is unit of randomization.	Karlan et al. 2010

Sector	Nature of intervention	Length of intervention	Time between start of intervention and end line survey	Main results	Sample size	Evaluation strategy	Evaluation author(s)
Education	Meetings to promote awareness about rights and the roles and responsibilities of school oversight committees.	Three rounds of 30 minute meetings in different neighborhoods of a village.	2 to 4 months	Different results in different states. Some evidence of improvements in teacher effort in two states, increased activity of oversight committee in one state, and modest to no improvement in learning in all states.	610 village clusters in Karnataka, Madhya Pradesh, and Uttar Pradesh.	RCT: Village clusters is unit of randomization.	Pandey, Goyal, and Sundararaman 2008

India

(continued next page)

Sector	Nature of intervention	Length of intervention	Time between start of intervention and end line survey	Main results	Sample size	Evaluation strategy	Evaluation author(s)
Education	3 interventions: 1. Meeting to share information about role of local oversight committee. 2. Identical to (1) + small group meetings to discuss learning levels to create report cards + village meeting to create aggregate village-level report card. 3. Identical to (2) + training of local volunteers to teach kids to read + 7 subsequent visits by NGO volunteers.	Several days	3 to 6 months	Oversight committees more informed about roles; not more active or knowledgeable about learning levels. No change in parental involvement with school, or knowledge of learning levels. No change in school resources, teacher attendance, or student attendance. Modest average effect on basic literacy skills only for intervention 3.	280 villages, 316 schools, 2,800 households, and 17,533 children	RCT: Village is unit of randomization. RCT + IV: Intervention 3 is used an instrument for reading class attendance.	Banerjee et al. 2010
India							

	Sector	Nature of intervention	Length of intervention	Time between start of intervention and end line survey	Main results	Sample size	Evaluation strategy	Evaluation author(s)
India	Health and education	Information campaign about right to free services and responsibilities of service providers	Two 1-hour sessions	11 months	Vaccination, prenatal exams, and prenatal supplement consumption increased in treatment areas. Nurse-midwives were no more likely to make required visits.	21 districts; 1,045 households	RCT, Diff-in-Diff. District is unit of randomization.	Pandey et al. 2007
Kenya	Health	SMS reminders for taking ARV medication. Treatments varied frequency of reminder and length of message.	Weekly or daily reminders for 48 weeks	1 to 48 weeks	Treatment adherence higher for those receiving weekly reminders than for those receiving daily reminders.	431 patients	RCT: Patient is unit of randomization.	Pop-Eleches et al. 2011

(continued next page)

	Sector	Nature of intervention	Length of intervention	Time between start of intervention and end line survey	Main results	Sample size	Evaluation strategy	Evaluation author(s)
Uganda	Education	Newspaper campaign that publicized amounts and timing of school capitation grants disbursed to districts.	Multiple years	5 years	1 SD increase in information leads to 44.2 percentage point increase in spending reaching the schools (1.1 SD in spending).	250 schools in 18 districts; additional 170 schools added in follow-up	IV: School's distance to the nearest newspaper outlet instruments for newspaper exposure.	Reinikka and Svensson 2011
United States	Social protection	Payday borrowers receive information about financial implications of borrowing against future paychecks. Treatment variants include presenting the borrowing costs and other forms of credit in comparable terms (interest rates and dollars), tabulating accumulated fees for hypothetical durations of	Time taken to read leaflets after taking a loan	4 months	Comparison of costs of different credit sources decreases payday borrowing. Comparisons in dollar terms more effective than comparing APRs. Repayment profiles decrease payday borrowing. Suggestions for savings have no impact on borrowing.	6,640 borrowers from 100 stores of a national payday lending chain	RCT: Store-day combination is unit of randomization.	Betrand and Morse 2010

Sector	Nature of intervention	Length of intervention	Time between start of intervention and end line survey	Main results	Sample size	Evaluation strategy	Evaluation author(s)
	outstanding loans, presenting typical repayment profiles of borrowers, and suggesting areas for budget cuts.						
United States	Education Low- and middle-income tax filers given information about personal financial aid eligibility and tuition rates of nearby colleges. Treatment variants include whether or not forms filled out on site and mailed immediately.	Normal session with tax filing service. Treatment variant with form filled and mailed on site takes an additional 10 minutes.	Within 10 months	No effect of eligibility information. Further assistance with financial aid application increases chances of filing aid application, and aid receipt by 15.7 percentage points.	26,168 potential students or their parents	RCT: Potential student is unit of randomization.	Bettinger et al. 2009

(continued next page)

	Sector	Nature of intervention	Length of intervention	Time between start of intervention and end line survey	Main results	Sample size	Evaluation strategy	Evaluation author(s)
United States	Health	University students given information on benefits of a tetanus inocula- tion. Treatment variants included fear-intensity of message and specific action plan for getting inoculation (for example, planned date and time of inoculation).	Time taken to read 7-page booklet	Intention to get inoculated mea- sured immedi- ately; actual inoc- ulation measured after 1 month.	Fear-inducing treatment increased inten- tion to get teta- nus shot, but pro- vision of specific plan increased actual rates of inoculation.	59 to 147 patients	RCT: Patient is the unit of ran- domization.	Leventhal, Singer, and Jones 1965

Sector	Nature of intervention	Length of intervention	Time between start of intervention and end line survey	Main results	Sample size	Evaluation strategy	Evaluation author(s)
			REPORT CARDS				
Pakistan	Education	Report cards on child, school, and village-level performance disseminated to parents and teachers through discussion groups.	2 years (2 rounds of report cards)	3 to 4 months (endline 1) and 15 to 16 months (endline 2)	Average test scores increase by 0.10 SD for public and private schools, and private school fees drop by 21 percent. Schools increase investments; households do not increase investments.	112 villages, 823 schools, 5,000 teachers, 2,000 households, and 12,000 students	RCT: Village is unit of randomization.	Andrabi, Das, and Ijaz Khwaja 2009
United States	Education	A 3-page report card on performance of nearby schools distributed to students in under-performing schools. RCT, treatment variant included 1-page form.	One time booklet in mail	2 to 9 months	Demand for other schools increased by 23 percent. Parents chose schools that were an average 0.10 SD higher quality than current school. No advantage of 1-page booklet over 3-page booklet.	Different evaluation samples: 6,700 to 10,100 students; 190 schools	RCT, natural experiment: Change in reporting about schools (100-page booklet without test scores to 3-page version with scores).	Hastings and Weinstein 2008

(continued next page)

Sector	Nature of intervention	Length of intervention	Time between start of intervention and end line survey	Main results	Sample size	Evaluation strategy	Evaluation author(s)
SCORECARDS AND COMMUNITY MONITORING							
Indonesia Social protection	Community involvement in targeting cash transfers. Households rank all other households in village by wealth in a meeting. The experiment included many process variants, such as presence of village elite, order of households for consideration during ranking, time of day for ranking meeting.	Community-based ranking took an average of 1.68 hours.	Immediate	Community-based targeting did not perform better than a proxy means test in targeting the poor. The community-based method is better at finding the very poor and generates higher satisfaction rates and fewer problems during fund disbursement. The community-based method targets well for households considered early in the meetings. No evidence of elite capture.	640 subvillages	RCT: Subvillage is main unit of randomization. For some process variants, the meeting is unit of randomization.	Alatas et al. 2011

	Sector	Nature of intervention	Length of intervention	Time between start of intervention and end line survey	Main results	Sample size	Evaluation strategy	Evaluation author(s)
Kenya	Education	Parents trained to monitor contract teachers and organize a performance evaluation.	18 months; 30 months		After 18 months, schools with trained parents had 0.2 SD higher test scores than comparison schools. Effect does not persist 12 months later.	140 schools (35 received training)	RCT: School is unit of randomization.	Duflo, Dupas, and Kremer 2010
Uganda	Health	Information on the status of service delivery and encouragement to community to monitor providers; providers given feedback on performance; interface meeting between providers and communities to discuss problems and possible solutions.	5 days	1 year	Increases in community monitoring activities (such as suggestion boxes), medical equipment, immunization rates, service utilization, child weight; decreases in waiting times, provider absence, stock-outs, and child mortality.	50 communities (50 public dispensaries) in 9 districts	RCT + Diff-in-Diff: Community is unit of randomization.	Björkman and Svensson 2008

Source: Authors.

Note: SMS = short text message; RCT = randomized controlled trial; Diff-in-Diff = difference-in-differences; IV= instrumental variable; SD = standard deviation; APR = annual percentage rate; ARV = antiretroviral. Refer to Gertler et al. (2011) for details.

References

Alatas, Vivi, Abhijit Banerjee, Rema Hanna, Benjamin A. Olken, and Julia Tobias. 2011. "Targeting the Poor: Evidence from a Field Experiment in Indonesia." Working Paper 15980, National Bureau of Economic Research, Cambridge, MA. http://www.nber.org/papers/w15980.pdf.

Andrabi, Tahir, Jishnu Das, and Asim Ijaz Khwaja. 2009. "Report Cards: The Impact of Providing School and Child Test-Scores on Educational Markets." Unpublished manuscript, Department of Economics, Harvard University, Cambridge, MA. http://www.hks.harvard.edu/fs/akhwaja/papers/RC_08 Oct09Full.pdf.

Banerjee, Abhijit V., Rukmini Banerji, Esther Duflo, Rachel Glennerster, and Stuti Khemani. 2010. "Pitfalls in Participatory Programs: Evidence from A Randomized Evaluation in Education in India." *American Economic Journal: Economic Policy* 2 (1): 1–30. http://pubs.aeaweb.org/doi/pdfplus/10.1257/pol.2.1.1.

Bertrand, Marianne, and Adair Morse. 2010. "Information Disclosure, Cognitive Biases and Payday Borrowing." Chicago Booth Research Paper 10-01, Booth School of Business, University of Chicago. http://papers.ssrn.com/sol3/papers .cfm?abstract_id=1532213.

Bettinger, Eric P., Bridget Terry Long, Philip Oreopoulos, and Lisa Sanbonmatsu. 2009. "The Role of Simplification and Information in College Decisions: Results from the H&R Block FAFSA Experiment." Working Paper 15361, National Bureau of Economic Research, Cambridge, MA. http://www.nber .org/papers/w15361.pdf.

Björkman, Martina, and Jakob Svensson. 2008. "Power to the People: Evidence from a Randomized Field Experiment of a Community-Based Monitoring Project." *Quarterly Journal of Economics* 124 (2): 735–69. http://qje.oxford journals.org/content/124/2/735.full.pdf+html.

Cutler, David, Robert S. Huckman, and Mary Beth Landrum. 2004. "The Role of Information in Medical Markets: An Analysis of Publicly Reported Outcomes in Cardiac Surgery." *American Economic Review* 94 (2): 342–46. http://pubs .aeaweb.org/doi/pdfplus/10.1257/0002828041301993.

Duflo, Esther, Pascaline Dupas, and Michael Kremer. 2010. "Additional Resources versus Organizational Changes in Education: Experimental Evidence from Kenya." Unpublished manuscript, Department of Economics, Massachusetts Institute of Technology. http://econ-www.mit.edu/files/4286.

Dupas, Pascaline. 2011. "Do Teenagers Respond To HIV Risk Information? Evidence from a Field Experiment in Kenya." American *Economic Journal: Applied Economics* 3 (1): 1–34. http://www.aeaweb.org/articles.php?doi= 10.1257/app.3.1.1.

Gertler, Paul J., Sebastian Martinez, Patrick Premand, Laura B. Rawlings, and Christel M. J. Vermeersch. 2011. "Impact Evaluation in Practice." World Bank,

Washington, DC. http://siteresources.worldbank.org/EXTHDOFFICE/Resources/5485726-1295455628620/Impact_Evaluation_in_Practice.pdf.

Hastings, Justine S., and Jeffrey M. Weinstein. 2008. "Information, School Choice and Academic Achievement: Evidence from Two Experiments." *Quarterly Journal of Economics, MIT Press* 123 (4): 1373–414. http://qje.oxfordjournals.org/content/123/4/1373.full.pdf+html.

Karlan, Dean, Margaret McConnell, Sendhil Mullainathan, and Jonathan Zinman. 2010. "Getting to the Top of Mind: How Reminders Increase Saving." Working Paper 16205, National Bureau of Economic Research, Cambridge, MA. http://www.nber.org/papers/w16205.pdf.

Keefer, Philip, and Stuti Khemani. 2011. "Mass Media and Public Services: The Effects of Radio Access on Public Education in Benin." Working Paper 5559, World Bank, Washington, DC. http://www-wds.worldbank.org/servlet/WDSContentServer/WDSP/IB/2011/02/07/000158349_20110207095259/Rendered/PDF/WPS5559.pdf.

Leventhal Howard, Robert Singer, and Susan Jones. 1965. "Effects of Fear and Specificity of Recommendation upon Attitudes and Behavior." *Journal of Personality and Social Psychology* 34: 20–29. http://www.sciencedirect.com/science/article/pii/S0022351407607353.

Pandey, Priyanaka, Sangeeta Goyal, and Venkatesh Sundararaman. 2008. "Community Participation in Public Schools: The Impact of Information Campaigns in Three Indian States." Unpublished manuscript, World Bank, Washington, DC. http://www-wds.worldbank.org/external/default/WDSContentServer/IW3P/IB/2008/11/11/000158349_20081111142153/Rendered/PDF/WPS4776.pdf.

Pandey, Priyanka, Ashwini R. Sehgal, Michelle Riboud, David Levine, and Madhav Goyal. 2007. "Informing Resource Poor Populations and the Delivery of Entitled Health and Social Services in Rural India." *Journal of the American Medical Association* 298 (16): 1867–75. http://jama.ama-assn.org/content/298/16/1867.full.pdf.

Pop-Eleches, Cristian, Harsha Thirumurthy, James P. Habyarimana, Joshua G. Zivin, Markus P. Goldstein, Damien de Walque, Leslie MacKeen, Jessica Haberer, Sylvester Kimaiyo, John Sidle, Duncan Ngare, and David R. Bangsberg. 2011. "Mobile Phone Technologies Improve Adherence to Antiretroviral Treatment in a Resource Limited Setting: A Randomized Controlled Trial of Text Message Reminders." *AIDS* 25 (6): 825–34. http://journals.lww.com/aidsonline/Abstract/2011/03270/Mobile_phone_technologies_improve_adherence_to.13.aspx.

Reinikka, Ritva, and Jakon Svensson. 2011. "The Power of Information in Public Services: Evidence from Education in Uganda." *Journal of Public Economics* 95 (7–8): 956–966.

www.ingramcontent.com/pod-product-compliance
Lightning Source LLC
Chambersburg PA
CBHW061748270326
41928CB00011B/2419